CW00341082

Canterbury
A Second Selection
IN OLD PHOTOGRAPHS

George Robert Barrett's cycle and motor business at 30 St Peter's Street in the 1930s. The business was established in 1902 in premises formerly used by Canterbury and District Co-operative Society Ltd. The attractive building stood opposite St Peter's Place and carried advertisements showing that Barrett's were official agents for Humber and Rover cars. In due course they also became agents for Austin cars and were much involved in BSA cycles. In 1933, when a newspaper photograph showed fifty BSA cycles being unloaded at the premises, you could buy one for 2s 2d a week. Enemy action in 1944 badly damaged the garage but the business survived and in the post-war years sold not only cars but toys, radios, cycles, records, prams, nursery furniture and electrical goods. George Barrett became mayor of Canterbury in 1927 and was elected alderman in 1938. His son, John R. Barrett, also held the post of mayor in 1952. A few years ago the premises were re-developed, in keeping with their 1930s appearance.

Canterbury

A Second Selection

IN OLD PHOTOGRAPHS

Compiled by DEREK BUTLER

Alan Sutton Publishing Limited
Phoenix Mill · Far Thrupp
Stroud · Gloucestershire

ALAN
SUTTON

First Published 1993

Copyright © Derek Butler

This book is dedicated to the memory of Robert
H. Brown, a friend and colleague who loved
Canterbury.

British Library Cataloguing in Publication Data

Butler, Derek
  Canterbury in Old Photographs: Second
  Selection
  I. Title
  942.234
  ISBN 0-7509-0399-6

Typeset in 9/10 Sabon.
Typesetting and origination by
Alan Sutton Publishing Limited
Printed in Great Britain by
Redwood Books, Trowbridge.

Contents

Introduction   7

1. Events   9

2. Shops and Hotels   31

3. Commercial and Agricultural Life   55

4. The Churches   77

5. Sport and Leisure   85

6. Streets and Buildings   99

7. Schools   131

8. The Second World War   143

9. People   151

Acknowledgements   160

The Central Picture Theatre, 1927. Commonly known as the 'Central', the theatre was designed by Harold Anderson of Dore & Anderson, 25 Watling Street, Canterbury, and opened in 1927. Built on the site of the former St Margaret's Hall, the cinema had seating for over 700 people who first enjoyed the silent films of the day followed by the 'talkies' of the 1930s. Following the blitz of June 1942, when a number of properties in St Margaret's Street were badly damaged, the cinema had to close for some months. A stark advertisement in the *Kentish Gazette* of 6 June 1942 announced 'Temporarily Closed – Re-opening Shortly'. A fervent cinema-goer from schoolboy days, especially as a member of the Odeon Saturday morning club, I enjoyed many a film at the Central, which was rather a poor relation to the Odeon and Regal cinemas.

Introduction

The interest shown in my first publication of old photographs four years ago prompted me to attempt a 'second selection', which I hope will appeal not only to those residents who have lived in the city for many years but also to those who have made their home in Canterbury during its expansion over the past twenty-five years or so. Once again I have drawn largely upon my own collection of picture postcards and other material which I have assembled over the past fifteen years, although I have also included photographs loaned to me by friends and relatives. As in the previous book a good deal of the material derives from the output of the three local photographic studios – Frank Bailey, John G. Charlton and B. & W. Fisk-Moore. The work of other local photographers is also featured to some extent – Ackland & Youngman, H.B. Collis, J. Craik, Wallace Mumford and D.M. Pinnington. Their record of life in the city from the turn of the century to the end of the Second World War is unique for it was not until the 1950s that local newspapers employed their own photographers to carry on this tradition.

Much influenced by the Romans, the coming of Augustine in 597 and the subsequent building of the Cathedral, Canterbury became a centre of pilgrimage in the Middle Ages and countless thousands came to visit the tomb of the martyred Archbishop Thomas à Becket. Visitors are still coming to the city in great numbers to see the Cathedral and other ancient buildings and sites and also because of the attraction of its modern shops and department stores. The University attracts students from all over the world who wish to live in a modern city, yet which also retains buildings from previous centuries that survived Hitler's bombers in 1942.

For local citizens the events and happenings of the past sixty to seventy years are of great nostalgic interest, an interest nurtured by the 'Memories' section of the Kent Messenger's local newspaper the *Extra*. A mystery photograph of an event or group of people brings forth a speedy response from the public, with identification of locations, persons and additional information. The formation of the Canterbury and East Kent Postcard Club in

1980 and the reproduction of old picture postcards, for example, the Saunders reprints, have contributed to the pool of local knowledge, encouraged new collectors and also stimulated an interest in local history.

In this selection I have endeavoured to include a variety of pictures that reflect the everyday life of the citizens of Canterbury. They are ones, however, which appeal to me personally and reflect to some extent my own interests and connections with the city.

I am most grateful for the feedback which I received after the publication of the previous selection and for the new information and comment that was forthcoming. I am also obliged to numerous local people who have supplied me with information relating to the photographs used here and who have enjoyed the chance to reminisce about their friends and relatives, school days, work and leisure activities. As the years go by it is becoming more difficult to obtain pre-Second World War material and it is hoped that what does surface will be made available in some form or other.

I have very much enjoyed compiling this new selection, much of which will be new to many people. I hope that those who look at the book will experience similar enjoyment. As before, I have endeavoured to obtain permission to reproduce photographs which are copyright and I apologize for possible omissions.

SECTION ONE

Events

A Commer motor charabanc ready to set out on an outing from the Queen's Head (now called the Three Tuns) early this century.

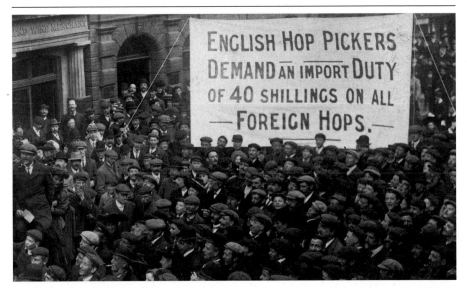

A demonstration outside the Corn Exchange in St George's Street during May 1908, in a protest demanding a 40s duty on imported hops. One banner displayed at the various meetings around the county and in London read 'And shall hops picked by Chinamen make England's hop trade die. Here's 50,000 Kentish men will know the reason why.'

The erection of a giant telegraph pole, possibly in the Wincheap area. The photograph, taken by Frank Bailey, dates from before the First World War. The eighteen-strong group of workmen are using another pole fitted with a pulley to help position the telegraph pole into its hole. At that time Frank Bailey was advertising as 'The People's Popular Photographer. Prompt and Pleasing Portraits. Permanent Prints at Popular Prices.'

The 'Canterbury Belle', a stage-coach drawn by four horses, outside the House of the White Swan, Northgate, early in 1947. The coach made regular trips around the local countryside during the summer months from the White Swan, which stands adjacent to St John's Hospital. A contemporary advertisement for the White Swan said 'from this old hostelrie the four-in-hand stage coach sets forth on its journeys to the coast and local places of interest, wending its way through the highways and byways, enabling the visitor to enjoy again the charms of old time travel.' Another advertisement referring to the White Swan said 'a building of historical note dating back to the eleventh century, with a tradition for the service of satisfying meals', and 'dine in a real old-world atmosphere, where, through the centuries, travellers of all classes have eaten and been satisfied.' The horses used to draw the stage-coach were stabled at The Paddock, Upper Chantry Lane, a site which now houses the British Telecom shop.

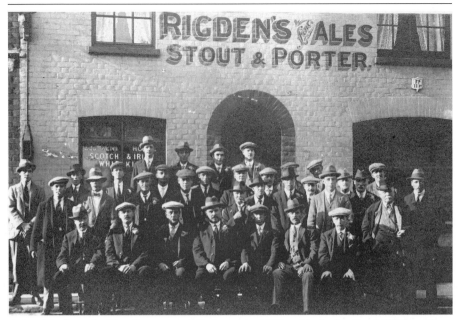

An outing from the Two Sawyers public house in 1923, with the landlord William Terry in the centre of the front row. Situated at 58 Ivy Lane, the Two Sawyers was owned by Rigden's, the local brewery, for many years before becoming part of Fremlins. Each of the men ready for the outing is wearing either a cap or a trilby hat.

A Dickens pageant procession in August 1933. Hospital funds were assisted by collections during the pageant. The stage-coach, discovered by Charles Yeoman, was used to convey the Dickens characters who included Mrs D. Brice (Mayoress of Fordwich) and Clifford Wheeler (Mr Wickfield). It is seen here outside the West Station. In the 1930s Mr Wheeler, who had shops in the Buttermarket and St Peter's Street, was largely responsible for producing a book blotter sold in aid of the Canterbury City Social Guild.

Engineer Henry Dawson, co-founder of the Canterbury Motor Co. in 1903, in his early monoplane at the Old Park in 1909. Mr Dawson designed and built the plane which was powered by a 30 hp engine, but recurring problems frustrated his flying ambitions. The aeroplane was later sold to Dan Sherrin, the well-known Whitstable artist. The photograph was taken by J.G. Charlton of Mercery Lane.

An Avro 504K biplane of Berkshire Aviation Tours at Thanington in the 1920s. For the princely sum of 10s you could go on a short flight over the city and duly impress your neighbours. The 'sole proprietor' of the plane was Mr F.J.W. Holmes of East Hanney near Wantage. The flights were made from a field near Cockering Road, Thanington.

The coronation celebrations in June 1953. The events included a fancy dress competition for the residents of Alma, Clyde and Notley Streets followed by a tea-party later in the afternoon. Among those taking part are Mesdames White, Whalley, Corbett, Owen and Mr Bromley. The children include Pam and Joy Gallagher, Terry and Tony White, Desmond and Vivienne Connolly, Alan Denny, Adrian Hicks, Brian and David Long, Philip Bunce, Janet Weller, Peggy Allen, Mary Burton and Monya Smith. The coronation queen was Joyce Hodgson.

A popular side-show at an event held at the Wincheap Athletic Grounds (later Brett's Sports Ground) during the First World War. The attraction was called 'A Ride in the Air', the cost of a ride being 1d. The rather strange contraption was photographed by Frank Bailey, who founded his photographic studio in Castle Street during the early years of this century.

Flooding in Pound Lane in October 1909. Some four inches of rain fell over a three-day period. In the background is Abbot's Mill, which stood at the junction of Mill Lane and St Radigund's Street. Pound Lane was to suffer heavy flooding again in December 1927 along with other streets close to the river.

Part of St Peter's Lane looking towards the junction with St Radigund's Street. Heavy flooding in the autumn of 1909 severely affected the St Peter's and Westgate areas of the city. Numerous photographs were taken at the time of the flooding and it seems that the residents were keen to pose for posterity.

The funeral of a member of the Municipal Fire Brigade in the 1920s. The procession is making its way along St Dunstan's Street passing the premises of H. Bateman & Son, builders and decorators, at Nos. 83 and 84, and the Model Bakery of William Peters at No. 82. At this time the fire brigade came under the control of the City Police Force. The present occupants of Nos. 82 to 84 are three separate hairdressing establishments.

The funeral procession of an AA patrolman proceeding along Westgate Court Avenue to the cemetery in the 1930s. Charles W. Lyons, the undertaker, can be seen preceding the hearse and other funeral cars. Until Westgate Court Avenue was partly developed for housing in the 1930s it was known as Cemetery Road. The cemetery, originally consisting of twelve acres, was opened in October 1877. An early report said it was 'well planted with trees and shrubs and laid out with serpentine walks'.

The Canterbury Fire Brigade in Castle Street in January 1926. They were called out to rescue a Persian cat called Rosie. Traffic was held up in the street while crowds watched Fireman Smith try to remove the cat from a 100 ft tall elm tree. Although he got near enough to clutch her tail she scratched him so badly he had to let go and Rosie dropped to the ground. Apparently none the worse she made a dash for another tree but was caught! The shops in the background are those of Frederick Baldock, greengrocer, at No. 50 and Henry Petts, confectioner, at No. 52.

An accident in April 1920 when a lorry plunged into No. 39 Northgate near the junction with Union Street. The local children were soon on the scene, as was the policeman, though not too much traffic control was required. The first three properties on the left were demolished after bomb damage in the Second World War, leaving the tile-clad building (No. 37) intact. For many years it was the grocers shop of Charles Barrow but is now an antiquarian and second-hand bookshop.

A very smart group, some with straw boaters, ready to leave on a charabanc outing from Longport. The old wall enclosed the garden of Bailey House adjoining the Cemetery Gate, one of the entrances to St Augustine's College. The photograph was taken by John Charlton in the 1920s. The charabanc may have been one taken over by the East Kent Road Car Co. Ltd from a private operator.

Staff of the East Kent Road Car Co. preparing to go on their annual outing in 1922. Three of the vehicles are Daimlers which were acquired in 1920 (reg. nos. FN 4334, 4335 and 4445) and are shown outside the Castle Inn, which stood at the junction of Castle Street and Pin Hill. The Castle Inn was demolished in 1963 so that the new roundabout could be constructed at Wincheap Green.

HRH the Duke of Kent inspecting a guard of honour formed by members of the 4th Battalion of the Buffs Royal East Kent Regiment under the command of Capt. G.H. Mount. The occasion was on 14 July 1937 when the duke, accompanied by the duchess, opened the new Kent and Canterbury Hospital. In his message to the assembled crowd the duke remarked 'I am sure you all feel very proud to have a new hospital which does honour to Canterbury, and is in a position to look after the needs of the County.'

The Princess Royal (Mary Countess Lascelles) inspecting a guard of honour formed by the King's School cadets in June 1937. The princess visited Canterbury to attend a service at the Cathedral for the Kent branch of the Red Cross Society. She presented new colours to the society, inspected the parade and took the salute at the march past of members.

King George VI and Queen Elizabeth visiting the city on 11 July 1946. They were shown the Roman Pavement at Butchery Lane, discovered in 1945, and were briefed on the pottery and other finds by Major F.W. Tomlinson, honorary secretary of the Canterbury Excavation Committee. This committee, formed in 1944, oversaw the majority of the excavation work carried out in the city at the end of the Second World War.

Princess Alexandra visiting St Edmund's School, on St Thomas' Hill, accompanied by the headmaster, William Thoseby. The princess came to the city on 1 June 1955 in her capacity as Patron of Junior Red Cross. In the afternoon she attended a Cathedral service for around 1,500 Red Cross cadets before having tea at the Red Cross Centre in Lower Chantry Lane.

A steam lorry pressed into service for John Hennicker Heaton during the election of January 1910. Mr (later Sir John) Heaton was the Conservative MP for Canterbury from 1885 until he retired in 1910 a few months after winning this election against an Independent Unionist (Francis Bennett-Goldney). Bennett-Goldney had hoped to succeed Heaton as MP but due to political in-fighting the local party could not agree on a candidate and Heaton was pressed to stand. His victory over Bennett-Goldney amounted to only twenty-one votes (1,371 to 1,350) and this prompted a further election in December 1910, which Bennett-Goldney won comfortably. Although Canterbury's population at that time was nearly 25,000 the city's electors totalled under 4,000. The lorry (reg. no. M 2319) is coming out of St Margaret's Street into the Parade and is well covered with 'Vote for Heaton' placards. The shop on the corner (later Hepworths) advertising flannel blankets and umbrellas was the drapers shop of F. & H. West and on the right is Finn's Stores.

A First World War tank presented to the city in July 1919. The mayor, Ramsay A. Bremner, with members of the corporation were there to receive the tank from Major-General Sir Colin Mackenzie when it was placed in the old moat between Rhodaus Town and the Dane John Gardens. The Guard of Honour was formed by members of the Buffs Regiment. Many of Canterbury's citizens witnessed this event from the Dane John Terrace from where John Charlton took this photograph.

Members of the Buffs Past and Present Association on parade at the old lawn tennis ground around the early 1930s. The tennis ground was located at the junction of Old Dover Road and Rhodaus Town and the association's headquarters were nearby. The ground was originally used by the Canterbury Bowling Club until its move to Nunnery Road in the late 1920s.

Customers of the Globe public house at 79 Castle Street about to leave on an outing in the 1920s. The Globe belonged to Jude Hanbury & Co. Ltd of the Dane John Brewery and survived until the late 1920s. It is noticeable that all the ladies are wearing hats and that men and women alike are sporting buttonholes. The building was demolished, along with the adjacent property of Cakebread, Robey & Co. Ltd, in the early 1970s and redeveloped for Crown Kitchens.

A 1920s outing from the Comet Inn. The inn stood in Broad Street quite close to the junction with Church Street St Pauls. The decorated charabanc is drawn up outside the main gateway to St Augustine's College and those posing for the photograph are attired in their Sunday best. The Comet Inn was a victim of the blitz in 1942.

The War Memorial to the Royal East Kent Mounted Rifles unveiled by Lord Harris on 15 October 1922. A great crowd gathered in the old cattle market and on St George's Terrace to see the event. Immediately behind the memorial are the premises of A.T. Bates (motor engineer and gun maker) and on his right Godfrey & Co. (pianoforte dealers), Pettit & Son (tobacconists) and the St George's Theatre.

The flags of HMS *Kent* deposited in the Cathedral 'under the keeping of the Dean and Chapter' at a special service on 1 July 1916. They were flown by the ship in the victory over the German fleet at the Falkland Islands on 8 December 1914. The flags were met at Canterbury West Railway Station by the Vice-Lieutenant of Kent, Lord Harris, and the procession was welcomed by the mayor at the Westgate.

The Mayor and Corporation officially welcoming a 1,000-strong party of French champion military gymnasts outside the Westgate Towers on 2 July 1907. The mayor, Francis Bennett-Goldney, is standing with the welcoming party on a platform erected for the occasion. The gymnasts were met at Canterbury West Station and were led in procession to the Westgate Towers by the band of the 1st Battalion of the Buffs. They then processed into the city led by the band of the 7th Dragoon Guards accompanied by a number of French bands. A special service was held at the Cathedral before the gymnasts moved on to St Lawrence Cricket Ground. Francis Bennett-Goldney was mayor for six years from 1905 and became Member of Parliament for the city in 1910 standing as an unofficial Conservative candidate. His election agent was his close associate, Councillor John G.B. Stone.

The residents of Thanington Road celebrating the Silver Jubilee of King George V and Queen Mary in patriotic fashion in 1935. In the city there was a full programme of events on Monday 6 May with special showings for schoolchildren at the three cinemas and a service in the Cathedral. In the evening there was a fireworks display on the recreation ground arranged by Barretts of Canterbury, a bonfire at Kent College which was one of a chain of beacons, and dances at the Drill Hall and Regal Ballrooms.

The town clerk, George Marks, reading the Proclamation of King Edward VIII on Wednesday 22 January 1936. Following the death of King George V, the Proclamation of the new King was made at various points around the city. This Proclamation at St George's Gate in the presence of the mayor, Charles Lefevre, members of the city council and the dean, Dr Hewlett Johnson, was photographed by William Fisk-Moore (see p. 153). Members of the Canterbury City Band provided the music and can be seen behind the civic party.

An East Kent bus en route from Herne Bay to Canterbury being held up in the Sturry Road in the early 1930s. Fund raising for the Kent and Canterbury Hospital took on various forms including Highwaymen Collections at points in and around the city. The passengers in this Frank Bailey photograph appear happy enough to be relieved of their small change for a good cause.

'Highwaymen' about to set off on a mission to relieve local citizens of their cash in aid of the Kent and Canterbury Hospital New Building Fund in the 1930s. During the years from 1921 to 1938 the Hospital Propaganda Committee was directly responsible for raising over £121,000, a remarkable effort given the economic problems of the time.

A Caledonian market held in July 1932 to raise money for the Kent and Canterbury Hospital New Building Fund. The old cattle market adjoining St George's Terrace was the venue for this event, organized by supporters from the city and the surrounding villages. A large amount of money for the fund was also raised via the Hospital Household Box Scheme, initiated by Major Henry James, chairman of the Hospital Propaganda Committee.

The *Invicta* engine being lowered on to its new base in the Dane John Gardens on 7 February 1969. For over sixty years it had stood just outside the Riding Gate after being presented to the city by Sir David Salomons. Built to serve on the Canterbury and Whitstable Railway, the *Invicta* was not a great success and was withdrawn from service after a year or two. It was removed again in time for the 150th anniversary of the opening of the railway and completely renovated by the Transport Trust at York. It is now on permanent display in the city's Heritage Museum in Stour Street.

Sturry Fire Brigade outside the premises of F.C. Snell in St Peter's Street. Severe flooding took place in the St Peter's area of the city at Christmas time in 1927. Some 400 houses were flooded and the mayor, Alderman G.R. Barrett, set up a Relief Fund with a target of £1,500. The *Kent Herald* printed a Flood Fund Appeal Souvenir which cost 6d including messages from the mayor, the dean, the proprietors of the *Herald*, J.A. Jennings Ltd, and the rector of Holy Cross with St Peter's. Fire brigade crews from the area assisted with the pumping out.

Abbot's Mill well and truly ablaze on 17 October 1933. The fire completely destroyed the six-storey mill, which was built in 1792. This photograph, showing the outer timbers near to collapse, was taken by a photographer from the local Fisk-Moore Studio. In 1983 the Canterbury Urban Studies Centre marked the 50th anniversary of the fire producing a souvenir publication containing contemporary accounts, etc.

A group outside the Cricketers Inn, 14 St Peter's Street, ready to go on a charabanc outing in the early 1920s. The name of this public house seemed to alternate between the Cricketers and the Kentish Cricketers over the past century but in the 1838 Stapleton's *Directory* it was called the Kentish Cricketers.

The staff of H.J. Goulden Ltd of Nos. 39 and 40 High Street preparing to depart on an outing, probably in the late 1920s or early 1930s. The outing was on a Thursday afternoon, the traditional half-day closing in the city. Many of Canterbury's older residents still talk of Goulden's with a good deal of affection. The business embraced stationery, books, music and fancy goods departments and closed in the 1960s.

SECTION TWO
Shops and Hotels

Mrs Ames and her son standing outside their antique shop, Memories, at No. 67 Burgate in the 1930s. The business commenced around 1930 and lasted until the 1970s.

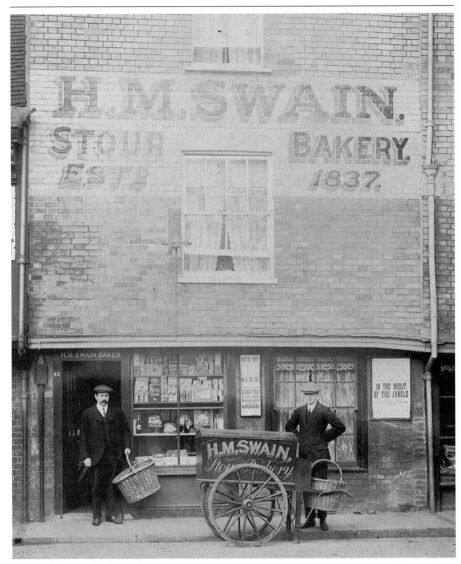

The Stour Bakery in the early years of this century. Established in 1837 by Herbert Swain, this bakery was located at No. 42 Stour Street, between the Royal Exchange public house (No. 43) and a general shop (No. 41). Adjoining No. 41 was Fortune's Passage, which ran down to the river and accommodated a number of small tenements as well as the actual bakery. In 1915 the shop was demolished prior to the development of St Edmund's Road. A new building was erected for the shop which retained its original street number. Since the Second World War the premises have been used as a general shop and more recently converted into a hairdressing salon. Advertisements for Rova Cocoa and Colman's Mustard appear in the window of the shop and on the outside are posters for *Week-End Girl* at the Theatre Royal and for the film *In the Midst of the Jungle* showing at the Electric Theatre in St Peter's Street.

Mr H.M. Swain's new bakers shop. The new shop on the corner of Stour Street and Edmund (later St Edmund's) Road replaced the previous Stour Bakery shop pulled down in 1915. Richard Swain (who took over the business from his father) is on the left, and in the doorway are his daughter, Dot, and young son, Cecil, in the arms of Aunt Nell. An employee with the delivery cart completes the picture taken soon after the shop opened around 1917. On the opposite corner to the shop was the Canterbury Cold Storage and Ice Works (not shown in the photograph), which was established around 1910. This business continued until the 1950s when refrigeration became more readily available.

The Home and Colonial Tea Stores around the early 1920s. The stores were originally situated at No. 36 St George's Street and were well established at the beginning of the twentieth century. In the shop window are advertisements for Perfect margarine at 7d per pound and butter at 1s 6d per pound. Tate & Lyle's Golden Syrup is priced at 6d per tin and tea at 2s per pound.

F. Sladden, confectioner and tobacconist, outside his shop in the 1920s. Mr Sladden opened his shop at No. 27 High Street around 1907/8 about the time the new post office was built. In the left hand window is a display of novelty egg cups (perhaps Easter eggs), postcards, etc., and also the *Canterbury Official Guide* at a price of 1d. On the right are advertisements for Carlyle tobacco and Hignett's 'Pioneer' brand. Mr Sladden continued in business until the late 1920s.

The Nag's Head, Dover Street, *c.* 1931. The first Nag's Head public house dates back to the eighteenth century but the one shown is the replacement built after its predecessor was demolished in 1930. The new Nag's Head was itself destroyed in the 1942 bombing raids and was followed by a further replacement in 1959. In its early days the public house was also called The Lilypot. Close to the old cattle market, it was a favourite inn for the many drovers who came into the city for the Saturday market. The Kent's Best advertisement on the inn sign is a reminder that it was once in the ownership of local brewers George Beer & Co., later taken over by Fremlins of Maidstone. The buildings on the left of the picture formed part of Holman Bros.' premises, who traded as engineers and millwrights in Dover Street for some 150 years.

The bakers shop of William Hopper, No. 42 St Dunstan's Street, as it appeared in the early 1890s. At this time members of the Hopper family had premises at five locations in the city. Mr Hopper traded in St Dunstan's Street from around 1890 until the First World War when Mr C. Phillips took over the premises. Over the years the name Hopper was synonymous with bread making in Canterbury.

Ye Quaint Tea Shoppe at No. 20 St Margaret's Street in the 1920s. Tea-rooms were established here during the First World War and continued until the late 1920s. The premises were adjacent to Finn's Stores and contemporary advertisements extolled their 'Scotch Shortbread' and other specialities of 'The Land O' Cakes' and 'Four course Light Luncheons for 2/-d.'

Loyns Bakery, with assembled staff, after the 1942 blitz. A few days after the bombing the *Kentish Gazette and Canterbury Press* carried an advertisement from Arthur Loyns saying 'Fortunately, the concrete bakery effectively withstood the fire, and as soon as the surrounding desolate area has been cleared, he will be able, aided and encouraged by the authorities, to again manufacture and offer for sale his famous bread and cakes. Providing of course that in the meantime no nocturnal visitor shatters his utilitarian efforts.' A few weeks later Arthur Loyns 'Extended a cordial welcome to all at his temporary shop amid the ruins of populous and popular St George's Street.'

The new Loyns Bakery at Sturry Road where it was built in 1955. Arthur Loyns erected his Machine Bakery, situated in Canterbury Lane, during 1928, a building which survived the 1942 blitz. As the site of the building was required for redevelopment, the bakery, now in the ownership of Nicholas Kingsman, moved to its new premises on the outskirts of the city. The 'new' bakery was itself demolished some years ago and now this site has been recently redeveloped to house the premises of Focus, Currys and MFI.

St Peter's Street on a sunny day just prior to the First World War. On the right are the attractive confectionery and tobacconist shops (No. 11) of George Heath and next to them Oporto House, the premises of Welby & Co., wine merchants. Beyond Oporto House are the larger gabled premises at No. 13 of Edward Lefevre the draper. It is pleasing that this part of St Peter's Street still looks much the same today.

The Kentish Cricketers Inn in 1954. Located on the corner of St Peter's Street and St Peter's Lane this inn is popular both with local people and tourists. Owned for many years by Flint & Sons of St Dunstan's Brewery (founded 1797) it later became a Fremlins (Kent's Best) house. On the left is the pork butchers shop of Ash (Kent) Ltd, and on the right St Peter's House can be seen in St Peter's Lane.

Collard & Son, wine and spirit merchants, at No. 37 St Margaret's Street in the mid-1920s. The extensive premises catered for both retail and wholesale customers. In 1878 the business was owned by George (later Sir George) P. Collard and retained its name until the 1930s when Thomas Carling became associated with it. The business finally closed in the mid-1960s and the site is now partly occupied by Reeves and Neylan, chartered accountants and partly (including some of the ancient cellars) by Alberrys Wine Bar.

The Oporto Tavern at No. 12 St Peter's Street in the 1960s. For very many years the premises were used by Welby & Co., wine and spirit merchants. An 1895 advertisement about Welby's stated that 'from the date of its foundation fully a century ago, this business has supplied the public of the city of Canterbury with the purest wines, spirits, ales and stouts.' The business was taken over by George Parr after the First World War but by 1930 the premises had become the Oporto Tavern with a much changed frontage. The tavern closed in 1969 to become a shop. In a nice gesture to the past the owner of the present shop has called it Welby's Bazaar.

ST. GEORGE'S WINE STORES.

Telephone No. 10.

WINE & BRANDY IMPORTERS,

BONDED STORES: Iron Bar Lane. OFFICE & BOTTLE DEPARTMENT: 43, St. George's St.

BLENDERS & BOTTLERS OF OLD SCOTCH & IRISH WHISKY.

H. MORTON & Co.,
43, ST. GEORGE'S STREET, CANTERBURY.
Price Lists on Application.
ESTABLISHED OVER HALF A CENTURY.

The St George's Wine Stores of H. Morton & Co. at No. 43 St George's Street. The business was established in the last century and the illustration dates from the 1890s. In 1898 they were advertising their own Scotch Whisky called 'The Record Reign' (Queen Victoria 1837 to 1897), which you could buy at 42s per dozen bottles or 21s per gallon. Their bonded store was situated in Iron Bar Lane. The St George's Street premises were destroyed in the 1942 blitz.

The Mineral Water Works of Mrs M.A. Robins at Malvern House, No. 89A Broad Street, established in 1865. A Canterbury guide of 1895 described the plant and machinery at the works as of 'modern character' – only 'the purest syrups, sugars and other ingredients are used in her factory'. Lithia, soda, potass and seltzer waters were manufactured at the factory as well as ginger beer, lemonade, orange champagne, raspberry champagne and lemon squash. The business did not continue beyond the early 1920s but the name lingers on through the bottles that survive. The photograph dates from the early 1890s.

Edwin Bing and Son, pharmaceutical chemists at No. 41 St George's Street, in the early 1900s. The business was well established in Canterbury by 1878. Through the years they particularly advertised Bing's Lavender Water ('Ellen Terry says it is quite perfect') and Lavender Soap. They were also well known as Table Water Manufacturers. The premises were blitzed in 1942 and the shop business transferred to No. 17 Sun Street until the early 1950s. It is probable that lavender water came from the Lavender Distillery at Grove Ferry where the Misses Bing not only ran the Grove Ferry Hotel but also the distillery.

A choice of bottles from two of Canterbury's mineral water suppliers. In a newspaper advertisement after the 1942 blitz Bing's Mineral Waters Ltd advised customers that 'owing to enemy action, we will be unable to produce any Mineral Waters for a time. Our customers will assist us greatly by retaining all empty bottles, syphon cases, etc. until we are able to collect.' As a child I was a great consumer of 'Bing'. Like many others I did not ask for a bottle of lemonade, I asked for a bottle of 'Bing' – either white or red. The taste was certainly unique.

FREDK. FINN & SONS, LTD.

ESTAB'D. PRIOR TO 1745.

FINN

THE CANTERBURY & EAST KENT STORES

BEST GOODS IN ALL DEPARTMENTS AT LOWEST PRICES.

ORDERS COLLECTED.   FREE DELIVERY BY OWN VANS.

General Orders of £2 carriage paid by S. E. & L. C. & D. Railways.

Do.   10/-   do.   by Carrier.

PRICE LIST GRATIS ON APPLICATION.

Post Orders receive special supervision,   *Articles not approved of can be exchanged.*

Telegraphic Address, "Finn, Canterbury."   Telephonic Address, No. 18.

22, 23 & 24, ST. MARGARET'S STREET, CANTERBURY.

An advertisement for The Canterbury & East Kent Stores. This was published in the late 1880s, appearing in a *Map of Environs of Canterbury*. The first grocers business was in place on the site by 1745 and Frederick Finn became involved in 1871. In 1885 the front of the main shop at No. 24 was rebuilt and the interior remodelled including the provision of an attractive gallery. In addition to No. 24, Finn's also used Nos. 22 and 23 St Margaret's Street to help house the various departments which not only sold groceries but lawnmowers, garden rollers, travelling requisites, general ironmongery, etc. In the early part of this century No. 21 was also acquired and this in time housed the toy and toiletries departments. For some years the meat department was housed at No. 45 High Street (The City Meat Stores), and the adjoining property No. 46 was also used by the company. In 1932 the business was acquired by Vye & Son, the Kentish Grocers, although the Finn's name was retained until the late 1930s. No. 24 St Margaret's Street remained a grocers shop until 1989 and is currently the Volume One bookshop.

The Bricklayers Arms in Best Lane with its
unusual inn sign. The photograph dates
from Edwardian times and the couple
shown with their dog are probably the
licensee and his wife. In its early days the
inn would have had strong links with the
bricklayer's trade; its name changed to the
Thomas Becket in 1970 when the city
celebrated the 800th anniversary of
Archbishop Thomas à Becket's martyrdom.

The Rose Hotel, at the
junction of the Parade and
Rose Lane, in the early
years of this century. This
attractive building was a
victim of enemy action in
June 1942. The adjoining
Fleece Hotel was taken
over by J. Lyons & Co.
Ltd, given a 'Tudor' façade
and used as a restaurant
from the early 1930s. It
survived the bombing and
continued as a popular
cafe/restaurant until the
1970s when it became the
fashion shop Snob.

Wootton's Stores at No. 78 St Dunstan's Street, formerly part of the old Star Inn, c. 1910. John Wootton took over this grocery shop from Charles Harle around the turn of the century and continued in business there until just prior to the Second World War. The reverse of this picture postcard carries an advertisement for Wootton's Teas. Mr Wootton was giving away a 'Bonus of Grocery and Provisions' in exchange for tea wrappers and one could obtain goods value 2s for ninety-six quarter-pound wrappers!

The 'Cheap Boot Shop' of F.W. Randall at Nos. 29 and 30 Burgate Street before the end of the nineteenth century. The business was established by 1870 and lasted to the early 1930s in Canterbury. Mr Randall's speciality was a horse-skin boot for gentlemen's wear, the uppers being made of horse skin and the soles of good English leather. A contemporary guide notes that 'although Mr Randall calls his establishment a "Cheap Boot Shop", cheapness it must be noted does not, as in so many cases, imply inferior quality of make or material.' The attractive double-fronted shop was subsequently used by various stationers and newsagents and now houses Lunn Poly Travel Ltd.

The staff of Burgess' Stores at No. 58 Palace Street in September 1950. From left to right: Alex Holness, Freddy Best, Arthur Goddard, Harold Gurr, Pat Spence, Joan Evans, Cecily Croud. Charles E. Burgess had two 'high class grocery and provision stores' at that time, the other being situated at No. 7 Mercery Lane. Mr Burgess took over the business from Mr W. Holmes in the early 1920s and his contemporary advertisement was: 'Collector and distributor of all the latest and newest produce brought on to the European Markets at London Store prices.' Mr Burgess' businesses were subsequently purchased by the International Stores, the Mercery Lane branch closed in the early 1960s and the Palace Street shop in the 1970s. Canterbury began to lose its independent grocers shops in the 1960s – in the 1950s you could still have a choice of shops in the main streets. Older residents will remember Burgess' Stores, Theobalds & Cooper (Buttermarket), Home and Colonial, International, Lipton, Maypole Dairy Co. (all High Street), World Stores (St Peter's Street), Vye & Son (St Margaret's Street), David Greig, Pearks, Pricerite and Victor Value Ltd (all St George's Street) and H.J. Flisher (St Dunstan's Street).

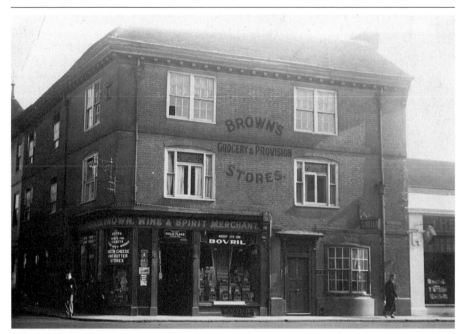

Brown's Stores at No. 24 Lower Bridge Street, at the junction with Church Street St Paul's in the 1930s. The business ran from around 1910 to the late 1930s. The premises were also shared by Mrs Brown, a corsetière for 'Spirella, The Queen of Corsets'. The building now incorporates A.D.M. Computing and the St George's post office. Part of the Invicta Garage can be seen on the right.

The staff of Dowlings, confectioners and chocolate makers outside their shop at No. 2 St Peter's Street, part of the original Weavers House. This photograph dates from around 1930, soon after the business commenced in Canterbury. When rationing began in July 1942, Dowlings' advertisement in the *Kentish Gazette* ran as follows: 'Dowlings are points ahead for quality, variety and service.' The business continued until the early 1960s.

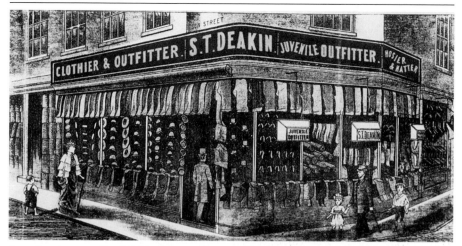

An advertisement for S.T. Deakin, outfitter, at No. 1 Sun Street. Samuel Thomas Deakin commenced trading in Canterbury at No. 18 Sun Street during the year 1856. The premises at No. 1 Sun Street, at the junction of Sun Street and Guildhall Street, were added some years later. This illustration was included in an advertising *Map of Environs of Canterbury* published in the late 1880s. In 1991 Deakin's of Canterbury celebrated 135 years in Canterbury and happily continue to trade in the city.

Thomas Tritton's shop at No. 37 St Peter's Street in the 1920s. A seventeenth-century house formerly used by Huguenot weavers, it still retains its attractive features such as the double door in the gable. The premises were a newsagents and stationers from the beginning of this century until the Second World War and were later used by Barretts Ltd as their pram shop. The poster on the right hand side is advertising the 'grand opening concert' featuring the 'Masqueraders Concert Party'.

Alfred Olby Ltd, builders merchants and ironmongers, in the early 1950s. This popular business at No. 25 Burgate Street was established in the late 1920s and continued until the 1970s. Before the advent of the large superstores, Olby's was the place to go for paint, wallpaper, brushes, nails, taps, washers, etc. It was also a good training ground for staff – both the assistants shown, Len Grace (on the right) and Colin Carpenter, went on to own their own hardware shops.

The St Dunstan's Floral Nursery at No. 89 St Dunstan's Street during the 1920s. A florists business had been in existence there since 1875 but by 1931 an estate agent had taken over the property. After the Second World War the premises were used by the County Laundry which later moved to No. 91. This enabled Lloyds Bank Ltd to convert Nos. 89 and 90 into their new bank in the late 1960s.

The tailors, Percy William Caister, at No. 14A Lower Bridge Street, *c.* 1930. The business was established in the 1920s not far from the junction with Ivy Lane and next door to St Martin's Rectory at No. 15. The Coplans family had a tailors business at No. 14 since the beginning of this century and Mr Caister continued the tradition until the 1930s when the premises were taken over by Needlecraft. The shop had plenty of stock when this photograph was taken – overcoats, raincoats, scarves, ties, caps, shirts and trilby hats all abound. The premises, along with others in Lower Bridge Street, were destroyed in the 1942 blitz.

The old Man of Kent public house with Edward Yeoman and his family standing outside in 1870. Originally two cottages, this seventeenth-century building subsequently became a public house. Edward Yeoman (grandfather of Charles and George) was licensee for a number of years in the second half of the nineteenth century. The Man of Kent was partly demolished in 1968 to make way for the second stage of the ring road.

Part of the premises of Barrett's of Canterbury in St Peter's Street after serious fire damage in 1937. The sales departments for cycles, radios and gramophones were most affected but a large 'Business as Usual' notice can be seen on the front of the garage. On the right is the Covent Garden fruiterers shop of Miss V. Lloyd. Seven years later Barrett's were to suffer more fire damage – this time at the hands of Hitler's bombers.

THE VAUXHALL", STURRY ROAD, CANTERBURY, (LT. SEYMOUR, PropR.).
MAIN MARGATE & RAMSGATE ROAD. SPACIOUS CAR PARK.
FULLY LICENSED. WHITBREADS BOTTLED ALES AND STOUT.

The Vauxhall Tavern, Sturry Road. The tavern was a useful stopping-off point for coaches going to Margate and Ramsgate, etc., in the 1930s. On this particular day it was a popular spot for passing traffic. Situated opposite the Barracks, the tavern had plenty of parking space for its customers. In October 1933 The Vauxhall was largely destroyed by fire. Mr and Mrs Seymour, the occupants, were quoted in the *Kentish Gazette* as saying that 'the interior of the inn was gutted and in the main part of the building on the ground floor the only part that seemed intact was the bar counter.' The newspaper also reported that after the firemen had been playing water on the blaze for some fifteen minutes the cat walked out of the front door! The Vauxhall was altered during restoration and received a more radical face-lift in the early 1980s. Among the coaches shown are those of the Premier Line and C.H. Betts.

The Buttermarket Stores of Clarke & Theobalds at No. 38 Burgate Street, c. 1912. The stores were established around 1909, taking over from The Cash Grocery Stores. Over the years the company's name changed to Theobalds & Studham and finally to Theobalds & Cooper, the latter carrying on the business until the 1970s. On the extreme left can just be seen the premises of Murdoch & Murdoch Ltd, piano and organ manufacturers.

Penn & Co.'s pram department in Butchery Lane in the 1930s. The Original Burgate Furnishing Stores of Penn & Co. were located at Nos. 45 and 46 Burgate and No. 16 Butchery Lane. The company was established in 1823 and it is interesting to note that John Penn of No. 31 Burgate was listed as a cabinet maker in Stapleton's *Directory* of 1838. In the 1930s they advertised a complete furnishing service and also supplied baby carriages. It seems as if the business did not survive the blitz of 1942, which destroyed the premises.

The butchers shop of Mr A.W. Clark at No. 51 St Dunstan's Street, around the beginning of this century. The shop, which stood on the corner of Orchard Street, is impressively stocked with all kinds of meat ready for the Christmas trade. There are notices showing the various prizes received at the Faversham Christmas Fat Stock Show and a reminder to customers that 'orders for prime English turkeys should be given early'. The premises are now used by the National Westminster Bank.

Mr and Mrs Thomas Wood outside their pork butchers shop at No. 9 Sun Street, early this century. The shop, which opened in 1899, has a tempting display of sausages and other cuts of meat and the inevitable butcher's boy with his trade bicycle. The Wood family played a full part in the civic life of the city: Thomas was Sheriff of Canterbury in 1905 and his son, Frank, was sheriff in 1929 and mayor in 1933 and 1934. In 1957 Frank's son, Peter, also held the office of sheriff. The business continued until the 1970s.

Ye Olde Northgate Curiosity Shoppe located in the premises of the old White Swan public house at 48 Northgate, at the time of the First World War. The shop commenced trading around 1912 to 1913. An array of antiques is outside the shop together with a notice saying 'This old Posting House open to visitors – no charge'. The proprietor was Valentine Sinclair and the business lasted until the late 1920s.

The House of the White Swan Restaurant in Northgate in the late 1940s. Further along the road can be seen the greengrocery shop of William Crippen, complete with a tarpaulin over its roof following bomb damage in the Second World War. Enemy action also caused damage to properties opposite the White Swan which resulted in the loss of 'Bourne Yard' and St Gregory's Square.

SECTION THREE

Commercial and Agricultural Life

A steam tractor of C. & G. Yeoman, Wincheap, in Rhodaus Town in the early 1900s. Charles Yeoman can be seen standing by the wagon and his brother, George, is the driver.

The fortress-like Star Brewery of George Beer in the 1920s. The brewery was situated in Broad Street at the junction with Burgate, opposite the Saracen's Head public house. The brewery was demolished around 1930 to make way for the municipal car park and widening of the road.

Part of the Dane John Brewery, Watling Street, founded by George Ash in 1772. Ash & Co's premises, shown here in the 1920s, extended over six acres including the yards, offices, stores, malthouses, hop stores, etc. Famous for their 'Canterbury Ales', Ash & Co. continued in business until after the First World War when Jude, Hanbury & Co. Ltd took over the brewery. In January 1936 the City Council agreed to purchase the site for erection of new Council offices though the *Kent Herald* reported 'that there would not be any move to provide buildings on the land for some time to come.' To this day the site remains undeveloped and is used as a surface car park; the new Council offices were finally built at Military Road in 1974.

BREWERY PREMISES AND MALTINGS NORTHGATE · CANTERBURY.

The Northgate Brewery of Johnson & Co. in Sturry Road, close to New Town Street in the 1880s. The brewery, established in 1854, was purchased by George Johnson in 1866 and it supplied a variety of pale ales, beers and stouts including Canterbury Pale Ale, Golden Pale Ale, Canterbury Light Pale Ale, Canterbury Luncheon Stout and Canterbury Extra Stout. These could be obtained in casks or bottles and there were daily deliveries in Canterbury and the surrounding area. As well as having a bonded warehouse near the Westgate, maltings at St Mildred's and a shipping office at No. 46 St George's Street, the brewery also had a London Store in Walworth Road. Daily deliveries in London were made by their own drays. In 1877 the company became Johnson & Co. Ltd and an advertisement in 1886 referred to the winning of a Gold Medal in 1875 (Paris), a medal in 1873 (London) and a diploma in 1881 (Hanover). The advertisement also read 'Recommended and Consumed by eminent Physicians in England, the Continent and the Colonies.' George Johnson lived at No. 1 Albert Place adjoining the brewery but in 1898 moved to Sussex after selling the business to Messrs Wilson and Towgood who changed the name to the Canterbury Brewery. The original brewery had impressive premises and covered a large area. From the 1920s onwards the premises were used for many years by Childs the jam manufacturers, followed by Apollinaris & Presta and Schweppes Ltd, both suppliers of table waters. The latter company continued there in business after the Second World War prior to R. White & Sons Ltd taking over. A number of buildings remain intact from the original brewery and now house the tyre depot of ATS and the Builder Centre.

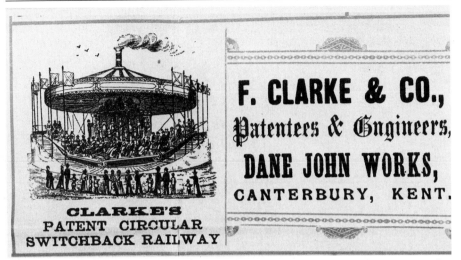

An advertisement for Francis Clarke's engineering business at the Dane John Works, No. 2 Rhodaus Town, in the 1880s. The advertisement is for his 'Patent circular switchback railway' but he also manufactured 'Col. Mackinnon & Clarke's patent canvas and steel targets'. His premises were on the site where the police station now stands, fairly close to the Canterbury Olympia Skating Rink and Kent County Pavilion, of which he was the secretary. The engineering business had ceased to trade by the turn of the century.

The interior of the Agricultural Hall at Rhodaus Town. The hall was built in the last century and was used for a variety of events and exhibitions. In this Fisk-Moore photograph dating back to the early 1900s the hall is bedecked with floral displays and garlands. After the formation of the Canterbury Motor Co. in 1903 the hall was acquired by them and incorporated into their premises. It now forms part of the workshop block.

Stephen Gower, a general dealer in waste materials who ran his business from No. 9 Hospital Lane, in the early 1920s. His advertisement in a programme for the Theatre Royal in 1920 read 'Best prices for all kinds of waste material – bottles, jars, rabbit and hare skins, old boots and shoes, old clothing and sacks, etc. Iron and metal broker.'

The Linotype machines in one of Canterbury's printing works, probably of a local newspaper. This photograph dates from around 1930 and was taken by Fisk-Moore. The mechanization of the laborious manner of setting type by hand was not solved in a satisfactory manner until 1886 when Ottmar Mergenthaler invented the Linotype, which as its name indicates, casts a line of type.

BLIGH BROS.,

CARRIAGE MANUFACTURERS

CANTERBURY, And at Preston Street, FAVERSHAM.

SHOW ROOMS

SUN STREET

100

Carriages in Stock,
Broughams,
Victorias,
Landaus, &c.

Designers of the
Canterbury Car
and Phaeton.

30 Medals Awarded.

SHOW ROOMS

SUN STREE

Near the
Cathedral Gate.

100

CARRIAGES

in

great variety

30 Medals Awarde

The Canterbury Phaeton built by Bligh Bros. at the beginning of this century. At that time the company's showroom was at No. 21 Sun Street and they boasted 100 carriages in stock, including broughams, victorias and landaus, etc. The Sun Street premises were vacated after the First World War. The phaeton had room for four persons and luggage and was 'light as a two wheel with all the advantages of four wheels.'

A vehicle used by James Clark & Son Ltd, who had their Kent Coast Glass Works at Roper Road. Established in the 1920s, the company manufactured 'bevelled, silvered, embossed, bent and brilliant cut glass, leadlights, ventilators and reflectors, etc.' They moved to Orchard Street after the Second World War and became known as James Clark & Eaton Ltd. The business remained in Orchard Street until the 1980s.

The Herne Bay and Canterbury double-deck bus outside Canterbury West Station in 1906. The East Kent and Herne Bay Motor Omnibus Co. Ltd was formed in 1905 and comprised a number of Herne Bay businessmen. The service between Herne Bay railway station and Canterbury opened in April 1906 with a Thomas Clarkson single-deck steam bus and this was joined by the double-deck, carrying thirty-four passengers, in May. The journey between Herne Bay and Canterbury took forty to fifty minutes and the single fare was 1s. Unfortunately the Clarksons were not a great success and the company folded in 1908.

Kingsford & Company's vehicle (reg. no. KT 7251) used for deliveries from their Barton Flour Mills in the 1920s. The Kingsford family was associated with Barton Mills from the eighteenth century until flour milling there ceased early in 1959. The mill supplied 'White Star Flour', and 'Aurora' was the registered trade mark for its self-raising flour. After flour milling ended the mill became associated with the manufacture of animal feeds. In the latter part of the eighteenth century William Kingsford 'exercised the trades of miller and paper maker in the parish of St Mary, Northgate'.

Folly Farm in the parish of St Stephen's soon after its purchase by Willy Lawrence in 1905. The 171 acre farm, including the eighteenth-century house, was on the market for £3,000. Mr Lawrence, with help from his sons, farmed it for forty-three years. Some hops were grown earlier this century but dairy farming become the main occupation. The farmhouse has changed little in ninety years though the surrounding area has been heavily developed for housing.

The dairy cart of Willy Lawrence of Folly Farm, c. 1909/10. In charge of the cart is Willy Lawrence's son, Guy, who later farmed at Sweechgate, Sturry. The beautiful horse and cart is complete with a large highly polished milk churn which could hold 17 gallons. Folly Farm is still farmed, albeit on a reduced acreage, by a member of the Lawrence family – Gilbert, Willy's great grandson.

Miss Minnie Tucker (left), Miss Annie Tucker (centre) and Mrs Kate Wood at Finn's hop gardens, Nackington, in September 1905. All three ladies, who were staunch members of the Salvation Army, seem particularly well dressed for their role as hop-pickers. At that time the Tucker family lived at St Lawrence Cottage, St Lawrence Road and during the August Cricket Week supplemented their income by storing spectators' cycles in a large shed on their smallholding and selling soft drinks to those going to the matches.

Part of Lillywhite's farm at Hollow Lane, Wincheap, in September 1935. The large baskets at the end of each row were called tally baskets and held five bushels of hops. These were checked by the tally man before being emptied into large sacks and taken off for drying. In East Kent hops were mainly picked in bushel baskets but old tin baths and other receptacles were also used. Canterbury was surrounded by hop gardens for many years.

The washing plant at Robert Brett & Sons' quarry at Riverdale Road in the late 1920s. This quarry, situated just off the Sturry Road, was formerly the brickfield of M. & F. Inge and survived until after the Second World War. Robert Brett started his haulage business in 1904 with a steam traction engine but soon developed into quarrying for sand and gravel, etc. The site of the quarry is now used as an industrial estate.

Two Leyland lorries (reg. nos. JG 7213 and NFN 308) belonging to Bretts Quarries (Robert Brett & Sons Ltd) at their Wincheap depot in the 1960s. The late Arthur Hammond was the sole driver of the older Leyland vehicle and clocked up 400,000 miles in it. The newer lorry alongside was its replacement.

LINOS Bros.   **Builders & Decorators,**   St. Dunstans' Canterbury

('Phone : CANTERBURY 1038)

Glinos Bros., builders, decorators and signwriters premises at No. 28A St Dunstan's Street in the mid-1930s. They were situated close to the level crossing and were between No. 28, the former station master's house, and four dwellings known as Railway Buildings. The premises that housed the four dwellings was formerly the National School, where the artist Thomas Sidney Cooper was a pupil early in the nineteenth century. Following raids by enemy aircraft in September 1940, all the buildings between the level crossing and Roper Road suffered considerable damage and were subsequently demolished. In the late 1960s the site was developed for use by the Marsham Tyre Co. Ltd.

A De Dion Boulton, reputed to be Canterbury's first motor car, built at the beginning of this century. The man sitting next to the driver is believed to be a Mr H. Williams, a tailor, who lived in Lower Bridge Street.

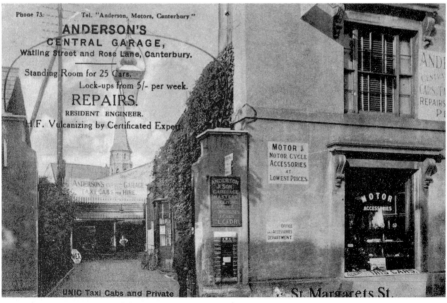

The garage entrance of Anderson's Central Garage in Watling Street close to the junction with Rose Lane in the early 1920s. Mr A.W. Anderson was originally the Riding and Job Master at the Royal Fountain Hotel in St Margaret's Street. The garage entrance was adjacent to No. 16 Watling Street. In 1930 the premises were used by the Post Office Engineering Department and later by Court Bros. The old St Mary Bredin church is in the background.

The Model T Ford delivery vehicle used by Messrs Theobalds & Studman of the Buttermarket Stores after the First World War. The van, in pristine condition, advertises the various departments of the stores. A few years later the Buttermarket Stores were advertising: 'Our cars deliver in all districts punctually and regularly. A postcard will bring our assistant to your door for orders, which will receive our personal attention.' How times have changed!

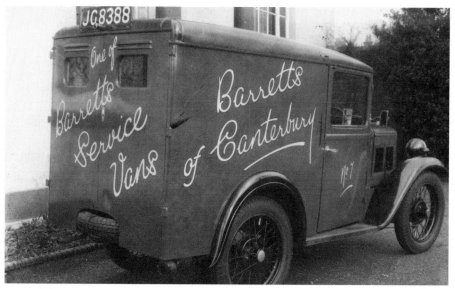

One of the service vans (reg. no. JG 8388) used by Barrett's of Canterbury just before the Second World War. The van is outside Westgate Court, Linden Grove, the home of George Barrett. In 1928 G.R. Barrett & Son could supply cars from Rover, Armstrong Siddeley, Morris and Morgan along with motorcycles from Triumph, Royal Enfield, BSA, Norton, Douglas, Raleigh, Zenith and Matchless.

Some of the vehicles of Abbott Bros. outside the dairy at New Dover Road in the Silver Jubilee Year of 1935. The vehicles as well as the shop are well decorated and the milkmen look very smart in their long coats and peak caps. The motorized vehicles were known as 'Fleets' and were basically a motorcycle with a small truck body built on to the frame. It is believed that the gentleman standing in the doorway is Will Sayer who was general manager for many years.

Milkmen from Abbott's Dairies depot ready to go out on their rounds in the late 1920s. The handcarts were equipped not only with the bottles of milk but also a full churn of milk and various measuring jugs. Abbott's Dairies were founded in 1786 at Limehouse, London, and moved to Canterbury in 1924. This family business ceased to trade in 1991 a few years after celebrating its 200th anniversary.

The *Duchess of Kent*, a steam traction engine belonging to Walter Amos Baldock, towing wagons packed with hop-pickers and their belongings in the early years of this century. Mr Baldock carried out his business of contractor at Tyler Hill near Canterbury and was much involved in the cartage of stone and gravel used for local roads which was quarried at Sturry. The wagons are outside the Bat and Ball public house in Old Dover Road, adjoining St Lawrence Road. The hop-pickers are probably on their way to Finn's hop fields at Nackington and are well loaded with their baskets, sacks, tin trunks, baths and chairs. The pickers used a variety of baskets and baths to harvest the hops, which then had to be placed in the tally baskets. The more experienced hop-pickers would ensure that less than five bushels was emptied into the tally baskets by tipping in the hops slowly and lightly – my mother-in-law was extremely adept at this! Those crowded on the wagons could not have had a very comfortable journey for apparently the wagons had iron wheels without proper axle bearings.

Canterbury's own power station, erected in 1898 just off Northgate. It had two chimneys – one built in brick and the other made of steel. There was some initial opposition to the provision of electricity from the local Council but when this was overcome supplies commenced in February 1899. The initial cost of the plant was over £7,000 and in 1899 the number of consumers totalled 193. In the first year of operation some 152,553 units were sold at a charge of 6d per unit for private lighting. The plant was upgraded in 1922 and again in 1929 and this equipment lasted until the station was closed in March 1959. In the 1920s the short road leading to the station from Northgate became Electric Road and three cottages, Electric Villas, were built. Just prior to the Second World War, Electric Road was given the name Kingsmead Road (meaning King's Meadow) when it was extended to join up with St Stephen's Road, following the construction of the river bridge. The chimneys of the power station were removed around 1960. The photograph dates from the 1950s.

The special tablet commemorating the official opening of the city's Electricity Supply Works on the 10 March 1899 by the mayor, Alderman George Collard. Other names recorded on the tablet include William Watson Mason, chairman of the Electric Light Committee, together with fellow committee members Frederick Gentry, Frederick Godden, Stephen Horsley, Edward Lukey, William Netherclift, George Pope and William Russell. I wonder what happened to the tablet when the works were demolished?

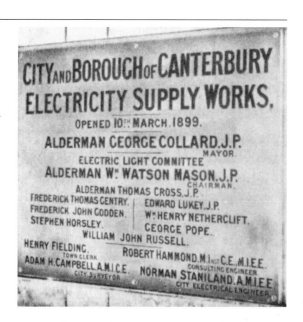

The engine and dynamo room of the Electricity Supply Works at the beginning of the twentieth century, photographed by H.B. Collis. The decorative balustrade lasted for the length of the station's service of some sixty years. The provision of electricity to the city's population was warmly welcomed and good profits were made in the first years which enabled new boilers and dynamos to be added. In their report to the full Council in May 1905, the lighting committee stated they were well pleased with their 10 per cent increase in current sold to private lighting consumers – an equivalent to 1,885.9 candlepower lamps!

A steam traction engine towing a very large boiler, outside the West Station in the 1920s. The engine belonged to Charles and George Yeoman who were established in the early part of this century as cartage contractors. They had depots at Tudor Road and Wincheap Grove and were also coal and coke merchants as well as household removers.

One of Yeoman's Burrell steam traction engines (reg. no. FN 502) in Wincheap before the First World War. The wagon is well loaded with timber, and Walter Yeoman, the younger brother of Charles and George, is the man standing alongside. An invoice dated 31 December 1923 shows that C. & G. Yeoman charged 7s 6d per yard for pit sand (delivered to Wickhambreaux) and 10s per yard for ballast.

C. & G. Yeoman's Dennis lorry in 1933. The lorry, used for their Express (20 m.p.h.!) transporting service from East Kent to London, is at the Wincheap Grove depot adjacent to the Canterbury Waverley Football Club's ground. Ted Yeoman, son of George, is the boy in the pedal car.

A Dennis vehicle (reg. no. FN 4845) loaded with hop pockets in 1928. The vehicle, surplus from the First World War, is at Yeoman's depot in Wincheap Grove, just to the rear of their office at No. 1 Wincheap (The Cedars). The company continued in business until 1949 when the transport operation became part of British Road Services following nationalization.

The trim shop in the old pavilion of Rootes Brothers' garage at Rhodaus Town in 1958. The Rootes brothers, William and Reginald, purchased the old Canterbury Motor Co. in 1935 and after the Second World War expanded their trim shop operation to employ some 250 people by the 1950s. Components were supplied to other factories in the Midlands but in the sixties production came to a halt and in 1969 Rootes sold out to Chrysler. Among the employees shown in the photograph are George Anderson and Henry Solly; the pavilion's gallery can be seen on the left. (Reproduced with permission of the *Kent Messenger*)

Beasley's Steam Dyeing and Cleaning Works at No. 22 Stour Street in the early years of this century. In their advertisements over many years Beasleys claimed to be 'England's Oldest Dyers and Cleaners' and that 'the Dyeing industry was established where Beasley's premises now stand in the year 1189.' The medieval house was badly damaged in the 1942 bombing and although part of it survived for some years it was eventually demolished and the site redeveloped. After the bombing a newspaper advertisement appeared: 'Blitzed But Blithe – the slight interruption in the 753 years of dyeing and cleaning on these premises *will be remedied shortly.*'

Canterbury East station in the 1920s. The station was opened in 1860 when the London, Chatham and Dover Railway Co. was extending its line to Dover. Two ancient mounds, similar to that of the remaining Dane John mound, were levelled to make way for the construction of the station. Canterbury West station, belonging to the South Eastern Railway, had opened in 1846 and now faced competition for the first time.

A steam train at Canterbury East station, *c.* 1952. By that time the roof over the station had been removed though a general upgrading of the station was still some years away. Milk was still being moved by rail and a trolley containing a number of churns is on the platform. Canterbury East saw its last steam train in 1959 when the London to Dover line's electrification scheme was finally completed. (Reproduced with permission of Peter Winding)

Subsidence in the Tyler Hill tunnel, which once served the Canterbury and Whitstable Railway. In July 1974 part of the tunnel began to collapse causing severe damage to some of the University of Kent buildings which had been erected above it in the late 1960s. The beginning of the subsidence under the Cornwallis Building resulted in part of it having to be cleared of furniture and equipment before it became too dangerous. I actually assisted with the removals and with other university staff witnessed the strange sight of concrete buckling as the building sank by a couple of feet. Immediate steps were taken to fill around half of the tunnel with a mixture of ash and concrete, etc., which was pumped through vertical shafts. The 828 yard tunnel was commenced in 1825 and when the railway opened in 1830 the carriages were hauled through the tunnel by a stationary engine. The last scheduled train to pass through the tunnel ran on 29 November 1952 with due ceremony but in February 1953, following the east coast floods, the line was reopened for a short period so that essential supplies could be transported to Whitstable.

SECTION FOUR

The Churches

William Temple (centre), who was enthroned as Archbishop of Canterbury on 23 April 1942. His chaplain, the Revd I. White Thompson (Dean of Canterbury from 1963 to 1976), is on the left and Canon W.E. Daniels is on the right. The photograph dates from 1942–3.

A group from the Queen Bertha's Home for Girls (No. 71 Wincheap) on an outing to Whitstable on 10 July 1911. The home, which was formerly called The Training Home for Girls, was run by the Church of England's Waifs and Strays Society (now called the Children's Society) and survived until after the First World War. The girls in the photograph look very smart in their summer dresses and straw hats.

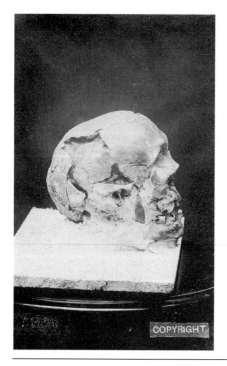

A skull reputed to be that of Archbishop Thomas à Becket. The postcard was published by photographer John Charlton after the skull's discovery in the eastern crypt in 1888. Becket was murdered in the Cathedral in 1170 and he was buried in the crypt. His bones were subsequently removed to a shrine in the Trinity Chapel until this was destroyed in 1538. Recent scientific evidence has concluded that the skull was not that of Becket.

The laying of the foundation stone for the present St Mary Bredin church. The Bishop of Dover, the Rt. Revd Alfred Rose, performed the ceremony on 31 May 1956. (I remember watching the event from my office window opposite the site.) Following the destruction of the old Rose Lane church in the 1942 raids, parishioners set about raising funds for its rebuilding and a new site was acquired on the corner of Nunnery Fields and Old Dover Road. Members of the City Council, on the right, attended including the mayor, Alderman William Bean, accompanied by the town clerk, John Boyle, Town Sergeant Roberts and the chaplain, Revd Alan Lawler. Among the councillors are Thomas McCallum (sheriff), Alderman Mrs Evelyn Hews and Alderman Harold Dawton. In the centre, with his back to the camera and notebook in hand, is the long-serving *Kentish Gazette* reporter, Mr E.H. Ovenden. The church was finally opened in September 1957. When there is so much talk today of poor attendances it is heartening to report that a new £275,000 extension to the church was built in 1993 to meet the needs of an expanding congregation and the local community.

The Salvation Army band accompanying nurses and Girl Guides, etc. in a procession along Roper Road in the 1920s. The flag is being carried by Mr W. Blanchard and the euphonium player in civilian clothes is band member Walter Minter. They form part of a procession to an annual Drum Head service in the Dane John organized by the Amalgamated Friendly Societies.

Members of the Salvation Army in full voice at an Armistice Remembrance Day service in the Buttermarket. The group is standing in front of The Buttermarket Stores of Theobalds and Cooper. The gentleman behind the trestle table is playing a squeeze-box and the lady at the front is poised to lay the wreath at the city War Memorial. This photograph, one of a series, was taken by Frank Bailey and dates from the early 1930s.

The funeral procession of a Salvation Army member proceeding along Whitstable Road en route to the city's cemetery. The Citadel's flag is carried by Mr Arnold and he is flanked by Jack Jannels (on his right) and Adjutant Albon. It is interesting to note that some in the procession are wearing white armbands and the ladies alongside the hearse have white sashes. This 1930s photograph was taken by Frank Bailey.

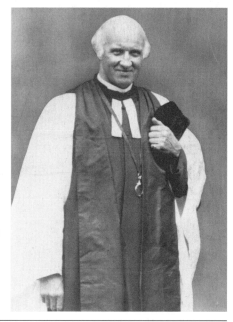

Dr Hewlett Johnson, who became Dean of Canterbury in June 1931 in succession to the famous Dr H.R.L. 'Dick' Sheppard. He had previously been Dean of Manchester, his birthplace, where his family had a manufacturing business, the Johnson Wire Works. After college he worked for a time at the Ashbury Carriage Works where, as he recorded in his autobiography *Searching for Light*, his slow conversion to socialism began. The 'Red' Dean retired in 1963 at the age of 89 leaving his large notice 'Christians, Ban Nuclear Weapons' intact above the deanery door. He died in Canterbury in 1966 at the grand age of 92.

The St Paul's church choir in 1928, a photograph taken by Fisk-Moore in the 'Choirs of Canterbury' series. Back row, left to right: Masters Keates, Austin, Linken, Wilkinson, Austin. Third row: Messrs Kerridge, Honey, Parker, Masters McDougall, Broyd, Jenkins, Vidler, Sturt, Ward, Messrs Wilson, Kennett. Second row: Messrs Chambers, Barrett, Watson, Woolgar, Alex Reid (organist and choirmaster), Revd J.T. Hales OBE (rector), Revd Arthur MC, Messrs Stanbridge, Saville, Theoff, Farrow. Front row: Masters Henning, Collard, Burt, Sutton, Kedge, Cooper, Harnden, Harnden.

Restoration work being carried out on the pinnacles of the central tower of the Cathedral in the late 1930s. The tower, 235 feet high, was known as Bell Harry after a bell originally given by Prior Henry of Eastry. Formerly called the Angel Steeple it was completed towards the end of the fifteenth century during the primacy of Cardinal Archbishop John Morton. In 1872 Bell Harry was rung when flames engulfed the roof of the Trinity Chapel.

The Deacons of St George's Place Baptist church with their minister, the Revd Vivian Evans, in 1948, the 125th anniversary of the Baptist church in Canterbury. Back row, left to right: Alfred Finch, Sidney Stanbridge, Leslie Newport, Maurice Kearin, Kenneth Lawrence, Charles Bentley, Stanley Ackroyd, Horace Hopper. Front row: Phyllis Hooker, Dr William Davis, George Anslow, Revd Vivian Evans, Alderman Frank Hooker, Charles Terry, Aubrey Moat.

The entrance to the old St Andrew's church in the Parade in the early part of this century. The church, rebuilt in 1774, was closed in 1880. Eight years later the parish of St Andrew's was united with those of St Margaret and St Mary Bredman, and the old church was used as a parish room. The gateway shown was built in the Renaissance style surmounted by a statue of St Andrew. For some years the entrance was used as a small tobacconists shop (C.B. Pettit) but in the 1970s the premises were incorporated into the adjoining Westminster Bank.

The Sunday School outing of the Broad Oak chapel during August 1905. The Countess of Huntingdon's Connexion Congregational chapel opened in 1867 and served the hamlet of Broad Oak, a few miles from Canterbury. Family and friends turned out in force to wave goodbye to the children and helpers who were accommodated on three large carts drawn by one of Walter A. Baldock's 'Fowler' steam engines. The outing was to Whitstable and in particular to Tankerton Beach where they parked near Peter Kemp's refreshment rooms. A few years later, Walter Baldock, the son of the owner, was unfortunately killed when the boiler of his engine exploded at Sarre while carrying sand from Broad Oak to Birchington. Broad Oak chapel is still very much alive and celebrated its 125th anniversary in 1992.

SECTION FIVE

Sport and Leisure

Members of the Canterbury Bowling Club during a West Country tour in the 1950s. The club was founded in 1897 and still enjoys great support.

One of the cup-winning bat and trap teams of the 1930s. Bat and trap was one of the activities of the local branch of the Buffs' Past and Present Association. This photograph was taken by Frank Bailey on the old lawn tennis ground at Old Dover Road, adjacent to the Buffs' headquarters. The Buffs, so named because of the colour of their jackets while serving in the Netherlands in the sixteenth and seventeenth centuries, became the Royal East Kent Regiment.

Regulars of the Two Brothers public house, including members of the cup-winning bat and trap team, ready for an outing in 1936. Situated at No. 91 Northgate and originally called The Spread Eagle, the establishment was closed in 1966 and remained so until converted into offices in 1992. The landlord, Edward Willey, is in the front row with his daughter, Vera, sitting in front of him, and his son, Ken, is to his left, behind the placard. The bat and trap team were winners of the Henry Court Charity Cup, an annual competition for the local league.

Members of the Canterbury Waverley Football Club soon after the formation of the club after the First World War. The photograph was taken on their ground at Wincheap Grove looking towards St Andrew's Presbyterian church at Wincheap Green. The chairman of the club, Captain H.G. James (Mayor of Canterbury in 1919), can be seen sitting in the centre of the second row along with other officials. Known affectionately as 'The Waves', the club continued in existence until the outbreak of the Second World War. During the 1930s the club also ran a side known as the Canterbury Amateurs, the senior team playing in Division 1 of the Kent League and the Amateurs in Division 2. The Waverley Football Supporters' Club raised funds in a variety of ways including concerts, boxing matches, wrestling tournaments and even grass speedway at Wincheap Grove. In July 1932 some 2,000 spectators witnessed a speedway meeting which featured the added attraction of local motorcyclist A.S. Bacon attempting to jump the nearby River Stour. Much to the crowd's delight he made it!

President:
H. G. James, Esq.

Hon. Treas. Sats.:
H. S. S. Amos,
82 S. Peter's Grove,
Canterbury.

Hon. Sec. Sats. :
C. H. Norton,
22 Prospect Place,
Canterbury.

Hon. Sec. Thurs. :
A. E. Finn,
23 S. Peter's Grove,
Canterbury.

Canterbury Waverley
Football Club.
Affiliated K.C.F.A.

Colours - - Green and White Stripes.
Ground - - - - Wincheap Grove.
Chairman - - - - H. H. Cooper.

County Mid-Week
Champions, Season
1921-22.

Winners
Kent Mid-Week
Shield (Thursday
Section), Season
1921-22. 1926-27.

Winners
Thanet Thursday
League Div. I. & II.
Season 1921-22.

Div. I. 1926-27.
Winners
Canterbury Charity
Cup, Seasons
1920-21 '21-22 '22-23
'24-25 '25-26.

Semi-Finalists
Kent Amateur Cup
1926/27.

Sir Stanley Rous CBE, JP, secretary of the Football Association, opening the new Kingsmead Stadium on 4 September 1958 in front of a crowd of 2,000 people. Prior to the move to Kingsmead the Canterbury City Football Club had played at Brett's Corner. On the left of the photograph are Jack Snell, the club's chairman, and Alderman William Bean, the mayor. Behind Sir Stanley are Mr G.R. Hews and the surveyor, John Mann. (Reproduced with permission of the *Kent Messenger*)

Members of the Kent County Cricket Club gate staff during the 1928 Cricket Week. The group was photographed by Frank Bailey in front of the 'concrete' stand on the St Lawrence Cricket ground. Kent's first game in the 1928 week was against Somerset and was the match selected for Frank Woolley's second benefit. For gatemen and spectators alike it was a frustrating day as rain prevented any play.

Canterbury City Football Club's players and officials in the mid-1950s. In the centre row are officials: A. Woodcock, E. Tritton, G.R. Hews, J.H. Snell (chairman), S.H. Loxton, S.H. Jennings, F. Butcher, R. Kent, C. Bates. The players include such favourites as Henry Brown, Tommy Francis, Bill Higgins, Bob Hawkins and Willy Craig (in back row) and Bobby Veck and Roy Evans (on left of centre row). The club grew out of the Brett's Sports Club and entered the Kent League in the 1947/8 season. For the first five years of its existence it was managed by Ernest Webster who was succeeded by Billy Walsh in 1952. The 1953/4 season was one of the most successful in the club's history and although Billy Walsh left to go to Grimsby the club beat Tunbridge Wells one goal to nil to win the Kent Senior Cup at Priestfield Stadium on Easter Monday 1954. Chris Bertchin scored the goal and skipper Bobby Veck accepted the cup in front of a large crowd including 3,000 City supporters. During that season the club also reached the final of the Kent League Cup, losing to Margate in the replay, and the final of the Kent Senior Shield which they lost to Sittingbourne. (Reproduced with permission of the *Kent Messenger*)

Members of the Payne Smith Old Boys' Cricket Club in the late 1950s. The Payne Smith School (named after Robert Payne-Smith, Dean of Canterbury from 1871 to 1895) was erected in 1895 and destroyed by enemy action in 1942. Back row, left to right: Brian Prett, Derek Matthews, Sid Ford, Ray Bourne, Roy Coker, Ricky Richardson, Fred Hadaway, Harry Sims (umpire). Front row: Wally Griffiths, Stan Burnap, Bernard Burton, Bernard Wenham. Bernard Wenham was also well known locally as an Association Football referee and, after his retirement, as a tireless worker for the Pilgrims Hospice Shop.

Canterbury Cycling Club members outside the Imperial Hotel soon after the club's formation in 1904. The Imperial in Martyrs' Field Road was the club's headquarters for many years and a meeting there in July 1946 re-launched it after its suspension during the Second World War. This meeting was attended 'by a large number of enthusiasts including many ladies' and a vote of thanks was accorded to Mr L. Elvidge, who had safeguarded the club's trophies during the war.

The Canterbury Male Voice Choir just before they gave a concert on the radio in July 1933. Their conductor was Alex Reid, who had served in that capacity for some twenty-five years. After their concert, which was broadcast to the British Empire, the choir adjourned to the Piccadilly Corner House where their chairman, Alderman G.R. Barrett, paid tribute to them and said that 'in honouring the Choir, the BBC had also honoured Canterbury, to whom they belonged.'

The Crotchets dance band who, under their director Fred Norris, were much in demand for local events during the 1930s. Towards the end of 1931 they gained second prize in a county-wide dance band competition organized by the *Kent Messenger* and are pictured here at that time. The band's members were Colin Turnbull (banjo), R.T. Sayer (drums), F. Williams (saxophone and violin), Fred Norris (conductor and pianist), W. Dutnall (saxophone and violin) and S. Ealey (saxophone and violin).

The Cantuar Dance Band, formed by local musician Eddie Newport in 1920. His musical interests were developed when he was at the Cathedral Choir School but it was not until he learnt to play the piano while convalescing in 1918 that his musical career took off. The group soon became known as Eddie Newport's Orchestra and by 1925 it comprised seven members with Eddie as conductor/pianist. The orchestra played at dance halls and clubs all over East Kent and had a popular following.

The cast who performed two comedy plays, *Withered Leaves* and *Checkmate,* at the Foresters' Hall, High Street, *c.* 1901. The plays were performed on two evenings to raise money in aid of the widow and six children of the late Postman Brown. The mayor and mayoress (Mr and Mrs George Collard) attended on one evening and such was the enthusiasm for the cause that on another night over two hundred people could not gain admission. A report in the local newspaper said that it was hoped that over £50 would be raised as a result of the efforts of the amateur company.

Joseph Daniel in the role of the 'Pirate King' in the 1922 production of *The Pirates of Penzance* by the Canterbury Amateur Operatic Society. The society was founded in 1906 and its first production was Gilbert and Sullivan's *Patience* a year later. Mr Daniel was headmaster of the old St Dunstan's School for over twenty years.

Canterbury's Electric Theatre. The theatre opened in 1911 and was situated between the King's Arms public house and Saunders' bakers shop in St Peter's Street. In 1923 the cost of tickets ranged from 6d to 1s 3d and *Just Tony*, starring Tom Mix, was one of the films featured. With the opening of the Central in 1927 the premises became Odeon Hall ('Concert hall and spring dance floor') and in 1936 the Canterbury Repertory Theatre. The Repertory Theatre's first production was *Precious Bane*, based on the novel by Mary Webb, and membership could be obtained for £1. 1s. After the Second World War one could dance every night to Frederic Hargraves' Swingtette at the Odeon Ballroom, which in the late 1940s became The Talisman Restaurant with seating for 200. The Talisman was an impressive restaurant and I recall being taken there on a number of occasions. In the early 1960s it became the Lok Yin Chinese Restaurant and more recently the Penguin Cafe. The photograph probably dates from 1911.

Opposite: The foyer of the Central Picture Theatre at the time of its opening in 1927. The dark oak panelling was in keeping with the general design of the building and is shown to advantage in this photograph. It is interesting to note that there are two Minimax fire extinguishers provided and the notice by the door to the stalls advertises two forthcoming films – *One Hour of Love* and *Pleasure Before Business*.

St Margaret's Hall, part of a complex that comprised the Freemasons Hotel and a smaller hall used an an auction mart. The main hall, situated at St Margaret's Street, was used for a variety of functions and in 1908 was the venue for two balls held in Cricket Week. It was used as an electric picture palace before becoming the YMCA centre during the First World War. It was then used as a billiard saloon as well as operating as the Empire Music Hall. The building was demolished in 1926 to make way for the new Central Picture Theatre.

The interior of the Central Picture Theatre in 1927. The 700-plus seats were padded but had wooden backs, not perhaps the most comfortable but in other ways entirely functional. The auditorium was decorated in Wedgwood Blue with the fresco work painted white, and the projection box was positioned at the rear. When the 'talkies' were introduced in 1930 the cinema was equipped with a Western Electric Sound System ('The Voice of Action') and patrons could enjoy a change of film every three days. In 1933 there were continuous daily performances from 3 p.m. with the added bonus of British Movietone News and an orchestra under the direction of Douglas Price. In 1934 performances started at 2.30 p.m. and the British Movietone had given way to The Gaumont British News. It seems as if the orchestra had also been pensioned off! If you went to the Central at the end of March 1933 you could have seen Norma Shearer, Leslie Howard and Frederic March in *Smilin' Through* – 'the most beautiful story every screened'. I recall seeing Michael Powell's *A Canterbury Tale* at the Central a few years after its première at The Friars in 1944. My school friend Leonard Smith from Fordwich had a major part in this film and I can remember the excitement of seeing his photograph in the foyer. The last film was shown at the Central in 1948 prior to its purchase by the City Council and its conversion into the first Marlowe Theatre.

Opposite: The first Marlowe Theatre. After a performance by the Old Stagers in August 1950 the theatre closed for extensive alterations including the provision of a new stage and dressing room block. The new theatre seated 480 in the stalls and 238 in the balcony and its grand reopening took place on 26 March 1951, when Terence Rattigan's *Love in Idleness* was staged starring Jessie Matthews. Tickets for the stalls at that time ran from 2s 6d to 7s 6d and from 1s 9d to 5s for the balcony. This photograph was taken either in 1975 or 1976 when productions of *Joseph and the Amazing Technicolor Dreamcoat* were staged.

The Friars Odeon after it closed as a cinema in October 1981, prior to its conversion into the new Marlowe Theatre. The Friars cinema was built on the site of Binnewith House and adjoining cottages and opened for business on 5 August 1933. Oscar Deutsch of Odeon was responsible for its erection but it was unable to have the name of Odeon in its title because of the existing Odeon Hall in nearby St Peter's Street. Built with nearly 1,300 seats including private boxes at the rear of the stalls, the Friars (later the Odeon) remained a most popular cinema until its closure in 1981. Along with my two sisters and brother I was a keen member of the Saturday morning Odeon Cinema Club and clearly remember to this day the serial *Junior G-Men of the Air* (featuring the Bowery Boys) which had us glued to our seats. I also recall that the toilet windows on the ground floor were conveniently placed for getting in the odd person who couldn't afford the 6d ticket! Fortunately, unlike its rival the Regal, which opened on the same day, it remained undamaged in the last war. When the application for a licence came before the City Council prior to its opening, Councillor Stone stirred things up by opposing the application on the grounds that the building was not finished. After a lively debate a provisional licence was granted subject to the building being constructed according to the plans submitted to the Council!

SECTION SIX

Streets and Buildings

Little Barton at Spring Lane during the 1930s. Built in the seventeenth century, the house was the home of Mr J.W.S. Mount for many years. Much of the surrounding area was given over to fruit farming.

An aerial view of the area around the East Station in the late 1950s. The houses in Station Road East, adjoining Pickford's warehouse, were intact as were those in Wincheap Green and Worthgate Place. The ruins of the Norman castle keep are on the left of the photograph and the gasometer in the centre. In the foreground are the houses built by the council in Oxford Road at the end of the Second World War.

An advertising postcard for the Norman Castle Hotel showing its position near the junction of Castle Street, Pin Hill and Wincheap during the early 1930s. The view also shows the Castle Hotel, demolished in 1963 to make way for the new ring road, and St Andrew's Presbyterian church, pulled down some years later. The advertisement reads 'There is every convenience and accommodation for motor coaches and motorists. We also cater for parties up to 50 persons.'

The railway bridge in Wincheap, by the Hollow Lane turning, which carried the old Elham Valley Railway. The cottages on the right are West View Terrace, built at the end of the nineteenth century. The premises behind the horse and cart were those of Alfred G. Lacey, florist and nurseryman. The bridge, which carried the railway to its furthest point at Harbledown Junction, was demolished in 1955. The photograph dates from the turn of the century.

The clearing-up operation at Longport after a section of the boundary wall to the old Kent and Canterbury Hospital collapsed in the mid-1930s. This caused some financial embarrassment to the hospital as a young lady passing by was seriously injured. The flint wall formed part of the original boundary of St Augustine's Abbey. The workmen have a brazier outside their rather ramshackle hut and a good supply of hurricane lamps.

The Canterbury Sanatorium or Isolation Hospital, which was opened on 25 November 1897 at Stodmarsh Road, *c.* 1904/5. It had room for forty-four patients and came into being mainly through the efforts of Dr Frank Wacher, who was Medical Officer of Health for the city from 1878 to 1928. In due course it became known as the Fever Hospital and was subsequently called Mount Hospital in recognition of the work of Mr E.J. Mount, chairman of the Hospital Management Committee for over twenty-five years.

The Old Mint at No. 37 High Street (Walter Cozen's shop) around the end of the nineteenth century. The stone cellar dates back to the twelfth century and the property formed part of the King's Exchange. Many British coins were struck at Canterbury in the thirteenth century, possibly in this vaulted chamber. The photograph was taken by Henry B. Collis, who commenced his photographic business around 1889 at No. 46 St George's Street, moving to No. 33 St Peter's Street at a later date.

Oswald House in Watling Street in the early years of this century. At this time it was used by Dr Thomas Soars Johnson for the treatment of patients with rheumatic related illnesses by 'Dowsing Luminous Radiant Heat Baths'. His advertisement at the time pronounced 'that the application of the Radiant Heat and Light Bath is unattended with risk or inconvenience to the patient. Its general effect is to prove soothing and to allay pain whilst the curative action is in progress.' It also mentioned that 'special accommodation has been made for the Artisan and the poorer classes'! Oswald House stood close to the Riding Gate but did not survive the bombing of 1942.

Dwellings which comprised St Radigund's Hall at Nos. 3 to 9 Church Lane, Northgate, in 1937. The rear of the building is shown before commencement of the restoration work undertaken by local builder Walter S. Cozens. Dating from the latter part of the fifteenth century, the timber-framed building was divided into separate dwelling houses for many years.

The restored building in 1938 before being used by the St Radigund's Girls' Club. After the Second World War it was used in turn by the St Radigund's Social Club and the St Andrew's Youth Club before being taken over by the College of Art's Department of Dress and Textiles. After the college vacated the premises in the 1970s it became the Radigund's Restaurant.

Longport Street in the early 1900s with its attractive trees on both sides of the road, a road wide enough to accommodate a market many years ago. The old Kent and Canterbury Hospital was situated behind the railings on the right (it opened in 1793) and opposite was the Payne Smith School, opened in 1895. The writer of this picture postcard has marked the entrance to the school.

A view of Sun Street from the Buttermarket at the end of the nineteenth century. On the left, at the junction with Mercery Lane, can be seen the Market Hall of J.R. Tomlin, wine and spirit merchant at No. 13, then Walker & Harris, the chemists at No. 12, William Hamilton, the optician at No. 11 (later to move to The Parade), Edwin Neame, baker and confectioner at No. 10 and at No. 9 the shop of T. Wood & Son, pork butchers. On the right is the draper's shop of C. Hatton & Son. Walker & Harris took over No. 13 a few years later and continued to trade as chemists until the late 1980s.

An aerial view of the city, *c.* 1930, complete with an Avro 505 bi-plane for good measure. Abbot's Mill, burnt down in 1933, can be seen on the left of the photograph with St Stephen's church, top left, in almost complete isolation. The two chimneys of the Canterbury Electric Light Works are just visible in the centre as are the barracks off Sturry Road. Little of the north-eastern part of the city has been developed at this time.

The cannon in the Dane John Gardens, photographed prior to 1914. It was taken from the Russians at Sebastopol during the Crimean War (1854–6) and was given a place of honour in the gardens which had been laid out in 1790 through the generosity of Alderman James Simmons. On 23 January 1943 the *Kentish Gazette* announced the imminent removal of railings in the Canterbury district to assist the war effort. These railings, including the cannon, were probably removed at this time.

The rear view of All Saints Court, an early sixteenth-century hall house which had two flanking wings added in the time of Queen Anne, in a photograph taken during the 1930s. Located in All Saints Lane and used as a youth hostel in the 1930s, the premises nearly disappeared in a clearance programme in the 1920s. It was restored through the good offices of Walter S. Cozens, a local builder who did much to preserve some of the city's more interesting buildings, as did his father before him.

The Barton of Christ Church prior to the Second World War. This was the store for the oats and barley used by the monks of Canterbury in medieval times. Produce was landed at nearby Fordwich, the port of Canterbury, and was conveyed to the local storage places by pack-horse or cart. This building stands alongside Barton Mill in Sturry Road. The doorway has now been bricked up and an additional window provided.

Church Street St Paul's looking towards Burgate in the 1920s. On the right can be seen the workshop of Tice & Co. and the confectionery and tobacconists shop of Richard Terry. On the corner of Burgate are the premises of the Star Brewery at a point where Broad Street narrowed to a few feet.

The *Invicta* engine. On this picture postcard dated 20 July 1906, the engine is being prepared for the unveiling on 8 August 1906. The building on the left is the Riding Gate Inn and the large house in Old Dover Road is The Limes. The latter was a victim of enemy action on 1 June 1942 and the inn a victim of progress. It was subsequently demolished to make way for a roundabout and the ring road.

A pre-First World War view of Hanover Road (now called Beverley Road) looking towards Forty Acres Road, with just a milk cart in view. Hanover Road was developed at the end of the nineteenth century and retained its name until part way through the First World War, when names associated with Germany were changed. The view remains almost the same today though it is unlikely that the road will ever again be seen free from traffic.

St Stephen's Road in the winter of 1909/10 showing St Stephen's House, which was originally No. 5. This house was for many years the home of the Revd G.J. Blore, headmaster of the King's School from 1873 to 1886. 'Blore's Piece', the King's School playing field at St Stephen's, was named after him.

The finishing touches being applied to some of the houses in Richmond Gardens, part of the Westgate Court Estate. This estate was completed in the mid-1930s and was built by H.V. Henshaw, who had his estate offices at No. 12 St Dunstan's Street, Canterbury. Suitable mortgages could be arranged by the company and there were some plots available for detached houses to be erected to the purchaser's own requirements.

An intrepid cyclist making his way along the middle of the Whitstable Road with no fear of being knocked over by passing traffic before the First World War. W. Pierce's St Dunstan's Nursery is on the left and beyond that the Wesley Manse. In the 1920s the nursery was taken over by Stanley Cripps, who continued in business there until the late 1950s when the site was developed for housing, viz: Ramsey Close, St Dunstan's Close and Somner Close.

The Westgate Court Estate, built during the 1930s, comprising houses in Clifton Gardens, Harcourt Drive, Richmond Gardens and Whitstable Road. The three-bedroomed semi-detached houses with one WC sold for £675 each, with repayments of 18s 10d per week including rates, and those with two WCS for £750 at £1. 0s 8d per week.

Houses in Clifton Gardens soon after their completion in the mid-1930s. Prices for terrace houses ranged from £575 to £590 and were advertised as having two reception rooms, three bedrooms, bathroom, WC, labour-saving compact kitchen and a good garden. All the houses were brick-built throughout with Marley tiled roofs and there were no road charges. Repayments were quoted at 17s 4d per week including rates.

Demolition work in progress in the Westgate Gardens in the late 1930s. The gardens, one of Canterbury's most attractive areas, were given to the city in 1936, along with Tower House, by Mr and Mrs Stephen Williamson. The house, which adjoins a bastion on the line of the old city wall, had two outer wings added in the 1870s but these were removed prior to the last war. The house is now used as the Mayor's Parlour.

Starr's House, within the Precincts, photographed by John G. Charlton around the turn of the century. The house was built by Thomas Starr, who served as Cathedral Auditor and Chapter Clerk from 1803 to 1840, and was destroyed during the June 1942 blitz. The name Starr is still preserved on premises at nearby Burgate Street.

The Prince of Wales' Soldiers and Sailors Institute in Northgate, established in the last century, opposite Coldharbour Lane. The photograph, taken by the Northgate Studio of R. Sinclair & Sons, dates from the first years of the twentieth century. In 1933, through the generosity of Charles Lefevre, the institute became the meeting place of the Canterbury Boys' Club and after the Second World War became the Prince of Wales Youth Club. The building was demolished a few years ago to make way for road improvements.

Jesus Hospital, at the Northgate end of Sturry Road, founded by Sir John Boys at the end of the sixteenth century. The almshouses making up the hospital are under the control of a warden. Sir John Boys, who was a wealthy lawyer, lived in a house in Palace Street, which was until recently the King's School Shop and the subject of many a photograph by visitors to the city. Sir John's tomb can be seen in the north aisle of the Cathedral.

Soldiers marching from Pin Hill into Rhodaus Town alongside the wooded Dane John Moat during the First World War. On the left are buildings on the Canterbury East station site and a wagon of the South Eastern & Chatham Railway can just be seen. The interesting building in the centre surrounded by a wooden fence has long since disappeared but the large building on the right, at that time Godden's Furniture Depository, still remains intact albeit serving a different purpose as a night-club.

A First World War scene with soldiers in Broad Street. On the left is the greengrocers shop of Mrs Marshall, though the soldiers may have been making for the bakers shop next door or even the Brewer's Delight further down the road. The house on the right, standing at the junction with Lady Wootton's Green, was known as The Priory. This house was another victim of the 1942 blitz.

Ye Olde Beverlie Inn and the nearby St Stephen's School in the parish of Hackington in the 1920s. The date 1570 is shown on a board above the main door to the Beverlie, which is not too far from the original ground of the Beverley Cricket Club founded in 1835. The St Stephen's National School was founded in 1848 and continued to serve the local area until a new primary school was built in the 1950s.

Sir Roger Manwood's Hospital at St Stephen's, at the beginning of this century. Sir Roger, who was a native of Sandwich, endowed the six almshouses in the 1570s. The parish clerk who doubled as warden of the hospital had his own house, adjacent to the almshouses, now known as Ye Olde Beverlie Inn. Sir Roger died in 1592 and is buried in St Stephen's church.

The Riding Gate Inn at the entrance to Watling Street, c. 1910. The iron footbridge at the Riding Gate, which replaced a brick one demolished in 1883, lasted until 1970. It now serves as a feature in the Heathfield Wildlife Park in Sussex. The inn, which was actually numbered in Old Dover Road, just survived the 1942 blitz and remained until 1955. It was eventually pulled down in 1969 to make way for the construction of a new roundabout and the ring road.

Longport House in Longport Street in the early 1920s. By 1931 the premises were being used by Dr F. Cassidi for his surgery, which was there until the 1950s. In the late 1960s the house was taken over by the Deaconess Community of St Andrew whose members served in the parish of St Martin and St Paul and in other local situations. When the community left some years ago the premises became a restaurant.

Ivy Lane House (No. 63) in 1909. In the early 1930s the property became Baker's Temperance Hotel and a new wing was added. The house now forms the part of the hotel (currently the Chaucer Hotel) on the left of the main entrance. In 1939 there were thirty-five bedrooms – bedroom and breakfast cost 7s 6d and a cup of early morning tea 3d. Prices for both luncheon and dinner varied from 2s 6d to 3s and you could have a hot bath for 1s or a cold one for 6d.

The property known as The Hall in Ivy Lane, before the First World War. At this time it comprised four separate cottages and it was not until the 1970s that it reverted to being one dwelling. This timber-framed house was the subject of a most interesting essay by Kenneth Gravett in a book, *The Parish of St Martin and St Paul, Canterbury*, published by the Friends of St Martin's Church in 1980. It is also fascinating to learn from the late Dr William Urry that Ivy Lane was once known as Beggars' Lane or 'Lodderelane'.

York Road at its junction with Martyrs Field Road from a picture postcard dated 14 May 1906. The peaceful Edwardian scene contrasts somewhat with the now busy junction and motor cars parked the length of the road. The corner shop became a private house in the 1980s but it has recently been converted back to its former role.

Wincheap Street in 1905 showing various properties which have since disappeared. On the left can be seen just a small part of the Royal George Inn (numbered 74 until the 1920s), with the bakers shop of Ernest Hopper (No. 73) next door. The house with the creeper is The Training Home for Girls (No. 71) and then comes St Nicholas Rectory (No. 70) and a number of cottages. By the mid-1920s the Home for Girls had disappeared to be replaced by Louis Elvidge's Wincheap Garage. The rectory and some of the adjoining cottages were demolished in the late 1950s to accommodate the enlarged garage premises.

The Black Mill at Harbledown, sited off the London Road in what is now called Mill Lane. The mill was of the smock type, working three pairs of stones, and from 1859 to 1892 it was owned by Charles Hancock. Fisk-Moore photographed the mill not long before it was demolished on 9 July 1913 due to its unsafe condition. After the attachment of wire ropes two traction engines belonging to Holman Bros. of Dover Street brought about the mill's demise.

A view of the Harbledown Schools (erected in 1852) in the early 1930s. Situated on the outskirts of the city on the London Road, Harbledown was well known to the thousands of pilgrims who made their way to Canterbury Cathedral to visit the shrine of the martyred Archbishop Thomas à Becket. It is interesting to note that the photographer, working for a postcard publisher, invariably included his Austin Seven motor car in the view!

St Margaret's Street, looking towards the Cathedral, at the end of the nineteenth century. On the left hand side are No. 41 (the tobacconists shop), No. 40, No. 39 (Miss Iron's Preparatory School where 'young gentlemen thoroughly prepared for public schools'), No. 38 (Bankruptcy and County Court Office – Walter Furley, solicitor and registrar) and No. 37 (Collard & Son, wine and spirit merchants). A horse and cart from the Canterbury Dairy can just be seen on the left of the picture.

The entrance to the Hales Place Estate at St Stephen's in the 1920s. This was between the almshouses of Sir Roger Manwood's Hospital and St Stephen's church, at the bottom of the present Hales Drive. Sir Edward Hales was the man who took over the Manwood mansion and subsequently built his own grand house in the mid-eighteenth century. This house, together with the buildings added by the Jesuit Order towards the end of the nineteenth century (St Mary's College), was demolished after the Jesuits left in 1928.

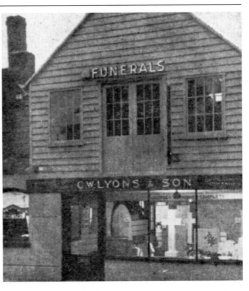

C.W. Lyons & Sons, undertakers and monumental masons, at No. 1 Military Road in the 1930s. Mr Lyons had a building business at the same address before becoming an undertaker. Lyons continued to use this property until the mid-1960s when they took over the former St Gregory's vicarage further up the road. The company is still very much in business.

MARLOWE · MEMORIAL THEATRE · ·

The Marlowe Memorial Theatre was the idea of the Canterbury Dramatic Society who at their 1932 Annual Meeting passed a resolution 'that an endeavour should be made to secure the interest of lovers of drama in the establishment of a Marlowe Memorial Theatre'. In March 1933 a public meeting at the Guildhall presided over by the mayor, Alderman Frank Hooker, proposed that a Marlowe Memorial Committee be set up. Lord Harris became its chairman and in due course plans were drawn up by local architect H. Campbell Ashenden. Although this venture did not get off the ground the city now has its Marlowe Theatre and 1993 has seen celebrations to mark the 400th anniversary of the playwright's death.

A Vauxhall Ten motor car parked alongside the *Invicta* engine near to the Riding Gate, *c.* 1938/9. When the car came out in 1938 it was priced at £168. Even in the 1930s vandalism was obviously a problem as the notice just inside the railings reads: '£1 reward will be paid to any persons giving information which leads to the conviction of persons damaging this engine. G.W. Marks, Town Clerk.'

A 1934 advertisement showing a Bentley sports car alongside the *Invicta* engine at Rhodaus Town. On the left is the warehouse of G. Twyman & Son Ltd, three dwelling houses and the Canterbury Motor Company's 'Skating Rink Garage and Pavilion Works'. It is interesting to note that around one hundred years separated the building of the *Invicta* (*c.* 1830) and the manufacture of the Bentley.

An aerial view of the Cathedral and the St George's area of the city in the early 1960s. The ring road had not yet claimed the Dane John Moat or the old cattle market car park and John Parker & Son Ltd still had their warehouse close to the roundabout adjoining the Riding Gate. In the centre foreground are the premises of G. Twyman & Son Ltd and on the extreme right is the large house St Bede's, at that time occupied by nurses from the Kent and Canterbury Hospital. For some years in the 1930s and after the Second World War St Bede's was a Kindergarten and School for Girls. During the late 1970s the building was demolished to make way for the new health centre. In the centre of the photograph is the bus station in St George's Lane. Preparatory work for the erection of Riceman's Store can also be seen alongside the bus station. This was opened in September 1962.

Excavations being carried out by the Canterbury Archaeological Trust in the Marlowe Theatre car park during the late 1970s. St Margaret's church, in the centre, dates back to the twelfth century and may have had Saxon origins. Following bomb damage it ceased to be a parish church after the Second World War though it was used as a Church and Institute for the Deaf and Dumb from 1958 until 1983. Following excavations by the trust the church now houses 'The Canterbury Tales' where you can experience a 'medieval adventure' based on a fourteenth-century pilgrimage from the Tabard Inn, Southwark to the shrine of St Thomas à Becket in the Cathedral. The theatre was demolished in 1982 and the whole area redeveloped as the Marlowe Arcade.

The junction of Watling Street and Rose Lane from Marlowe Avenue, *c.* 1950. On the right are the premises of the Kent Typewriter Co. and on the other side of Rose Lane is the general shop of H. Brewer, formerly part of Anderson's Central Garage. At the end of Rose Lane can just be seen Mr W. Williams' coach building business adjoining Philpot's garage. All the properties adjoining Rose Lane were subsequently demolished to make way for road widening, etc.

A busy St George's Street in the 1960s before parking restrictions were introduced. The block of shops on the left of the photograph includes G. Mount & Sons Ltd (florists), Dorothy Perkins Ltd, Scotch Wool Shop, Manfield & Sons Ltd, Mac-Fisheries Ltd, Phillips Shoes, Graftons (Gowns) and Bowketts Cakes Ltd. On the right can be seen part of David Greig Ltd – long since closed – and Woolworths Stores. The majority of the street has now been pedestrianized.

St Stephen's Pathway (on the right) and St Stephen's Fields in an early 1950s photograph taken from The Causeway. The block of houses in front of the chimney were demolished in the late 1960s but those on the corner of St Stephen's Pathway remain intact. Part of Hooker's Westgate Mill can be seen on the right, which was pulled down after a major fire in 1954.

Old Dover Road in flood after heavy rain in July 1953. It is now hard to believe that this photograph shows the bottom of Old Dover Road at its junction with Upper Bridge Street and Rhodaus Town. The fire station now stands on the left and the police station on the right of the entrance to Old Dover Road. Unfortunately most of the trees have disappeared. (Reproduced with permission of the *Kent Messenger*)

Dover Street in the 1950s, with Bradley's Agricultural Store on the left. Further up the street is the Beehive public house, now a restaurant, and the oast house, dating from 1811. The City Council of the day unbelievably gave permission for the demolition of the oast in 1959. In medieval times Dover Street was called Ritherchiape (cattle market) and its association with the market is vividly portrayed in a 1990 publication entitled *Dover Street Remembered,* produced by the Local History Group of the Oaten Hill and District Society.

Dover Street in the late 1950s, featuring the Star Garage of Bligh Bros. Ltd and H.S. Greenfield's gun shop. Bligh's took over part of the premises of No. 5 Dover Street, once used by Walter Cozens, the well-known local builder, in the 1930s. In 1960 Bligh Bros. acquired the adjoining cottages and built a new showroom and workshop. My first car was purchased from there in 1963. Bligh's continued to trade here until 1973.

An East Kent No. 27 bus bound for Thanington passing along Upper Bridge Street in the 1950s. Part of the old cattle market can be seen on the left of the picture. The No. 27 bus ran from Rough Common to Stranger's Lane, Thanington via the bus station, cattle market, East Station and Wincheap. The bus, reg. no. BJG 281, was a Guy Arab, which came into service in 1943.

Rhodaus Town in 1969 at the start of the second stage of the ring road, which followed the course of the old moat that ran around the city wall from Pin Hill. On the left are the premises of John Parker & Son Ltd, steel stockholders, houses at Nos. 3 to 5 Rhodaus Town and Rootes garage. The old moat area was an attractive spot and was once frequented by peafowl, which were often photographed on the *Invicta* engine. There was some criticism early in 1934 when the Council decided to sell the remaining eight peafowl for the sum of £5!

Houses built during the first years of this century at the lower end of Heaton Road. In the distance can be seen St Mildred's Rectory, which was demolished in the 1970s. British Legion flats were subsequently built on the site and were named Canon Appleton Court after a former chaplain to the Canterbury branch. It is presumed that Heaton Road was named after John Hennicker Heaton who was Canterbury's MP from 1885 to 1910.

The Oast House that stood in Rose Lane for many years, in the early 1950s. It was demolished when the redevelopment of Rose Lane took place a few years later. Prior to the Second World War it was used as a store. The Oast House was located around halfway between the old St Mary Bredin church and the Rose Hotel, opposite to where the present Trustee Savings Bank is situated. Close by was the entrance to Rose Square (at No. 5 Rose Lane), which accommodated eight tenements in the 1920s.

Construction of the footbridge from the Dane John Gardens, on the right, to the East Station at Pin Hill. The bridge was precast in sections and erected over a new part of the ring road in 1971. David Alexander, the photographer, included his Ford Anglia car in the shot. The bridge now gives safe access from Station Road East into the city via the Dane John Gardens.

Lower Bridge Street looking towards Broad Street in 1968. This photograph was taken from the roof of the Royal Insurance Office and shows the top of the Invicta Motors garage on the right and various buildings on the left which were demolished in 1969. At the junction with Burgate is the Saracen's Head inn, with its Fremlins signs, which adjoined the city wall. The building at the rear of the inn (No. 1A) is a Fremlins off-licence and the large house on the left, No. 1 Lower Bridge Street, comprised the surgeries of Doctors Gimson, Miles, Andrews and two dental surgeries.

SECTION SEVEN

Schools

Girls from the City Council School, St John's Place, with their Kent Music Festival Challenge Banner in the late 1930s.

Students in the garden of the Clough Secretarial School in 1954. The school, previously known as Clough's Commercial College, was situated at No. 6 Hawks Lane, St Margaret's Old Rectory House. Founded by Mr and Mrs J. Smith Clough, the college was later run by their son, Alan Clough, before moving to Folkestone in the early 1970s. Both Mr Clough Snr. and Mr Clough Jnr. can be seen in the picture and the students include the Misses Brown, Collinson, Danks, Horton, Ledger, Mummery, Stroud and Tyrrell. The lone brave male is Maurice Horn.

Girls at St John's City Council School showing off their prowess at physical education, around the late 1930s. The building in the background is the infants' school, which had its own headmistress and was run quite separately from the senior school.

The girls' entrances and playground at the City Council School in St John's Place, Northgate, which opened in 1903. It catered for 360 girls and 360 boys, whose entrances can be seen in the photograph, and 300 infants who had a separate building. The boys' classrooms were on the first floor and the girls' classrooms were on the ground floor. The photograph, by Frank Bailey, probably dates from the 1920s.

The private St Helen's Ladies School, located at No. 6 Ethelbert Road (old numbering), during the First World War. It was run by a Miss Young (ex Newnham College, Cambridge) and a Miss Lang and subsequently moved to No. 21 New Dover Road. Before the First World War schools for the 'daughters of gentlemen' were very much in favour. One such school in Canterbury's High Street also advertised that 'Little boys are also received.'

The Laurels school band, *c.* 1910. The school was situated in Watling Street and was described as a 'High Class College for Daughters of Gentlemen'. It thrived before the First World War and this photograph of the band, comprising violins and guitars, etc., is from its prospectus. A fee of fifty guineas per annum was charged to cover board, laundry, pew rent and the teaching of general subjects but there was an extra two guineas for piano and other musical instruction.

The St John's Board School in St John's Place, Northgate, *c.* 1990. The 1870 Education Act divided the country into School Board Districts as a result of which the St John's School was founded in 1876. At that time fees of 6d or 9d could be charged, as free education was not introduced until 1891. After the building of the St John's Council School in 1903 the Board School was used as the Council Cookery School and after the Second World War as the Canterbury School Clinic and Dental Centre.

Alderman Frank Hooker, chairman of the Canterbury and St Augustine's Joint Education Committee, presents a prize at the 1953 St John's County Primary School Prize-giving in the Chapter House. Nicholas Polmear, the Chief Education Officer, is in the centre with Doris Reynolds, the headmistress, on his left. The platform party also includes Councillor H.M. Kenny and Mr Reynolds. Frank Hooker, a local miller and benefactor to the city, served as mayor in 1931 and 1932 and gave his name to the Frank Hooker School (controversially renamed the Canterbury High School a few years ago), which was opened in 1956. A lifelong member of the Baptist church, Frank Hooker was a deacon at St George's Place Baptist church for over fifty years. He was elected as an alderman in 1933 and in 1951 was made an Honorary Freeman of the City. (Reproduced by kind permission of the *Kent Messenger*)

A class at the Simon Langton Boys' School in the 1930s with part of the old school buildings in the background. Following the 1944 Education Act fees were abolished and the September 1945 intake, of which I was one, was the first under the new voluntary controlled status, entrance being by examination. My year was also the last to take the old General School Certificate in 1950.

The Simon Langton Boys' School after the 1942 blitz. Both the boys' and girls' schools were severely damaged but a surface air-raid shelter is intact. In a publication *Front-Line School*, published at the end of the war, the headmaster, Mr L.W. Myers, wrote these words: 'We work still amid ruin and rubble, and if, presently, we may hope at least for tidiness and some extra rooms, we must, I fear, put aside for some years to come the hopes of that long-promised new school. So many national needs must be met before our turn comes. It is in these buildings and on this site that we have to make good our losses, to strive to give to coming generations not less but more than we did in pre-war days.' Five years after Mr Myers retired the new school finally opened in 1959, built on part of the playing fields at Nackington Road.

The staff of the Simon Langton Boys' School at the end of the Second World War. Back row, left to right: Messrs Pinnock, Gay, Hummerstone, McCulloch, McDonald. Middle row: Mr Reid, Miss Frampton, Mrs Morley, Mrs Hines, Miss Smith, Mrs Thomas, Messrs Ward, Humphrey, Cockerill, Byers. Front row: Messrs Owen, Smith, Tucker, Thomas, Myers (headmaster), Sharman, Fagg, Hall.

The gymnasium of the Simon Langton Boys' School, *c.* 1920. The gymnasium formed part of the New Wing, opened in 1914, which ran parallel with St George's Lane. The apparatus was still intact in 1945 and I cannot say that climbing the ropes was something I looked forward to. I did, however, enjoy the weekly trek to Nackington Road for the sports afternoon – soccer and cross-country running in the winter and cricket, tennis and athletics in the summer. Mr R. 'Jimmy' Gay, an LTA professional, was the PE teacher during my time at the Langton.

The staff of St Dunstan's (C. of E.) Modern School in 1956/7. Back row, left to right: Mr Gough, Derwent Wilks, Bill Haynes, John Brisley, Ron Skinner, Eric Croucher. Front row: -?-, Ken Harding, Eric Manthorpe, Ronald Ratledge (headmaster), Denis Reding, Reginald Hake, Charles Day. The St Dunstan's Parochial School was erected in 1862 on a site in London Road adjacent to St Dunstan's Terrace and next door to Westgate Court Farm. It had room for a total of 234 pupils divided into boys, girls and infants. After the Second World War it became a Modern School for boys but closed in the summer of 1957 when it became part of the new Archbishop's Secondary School. Mr Ratledge became the headmaster of the new school and a number of the above staff joined him there.

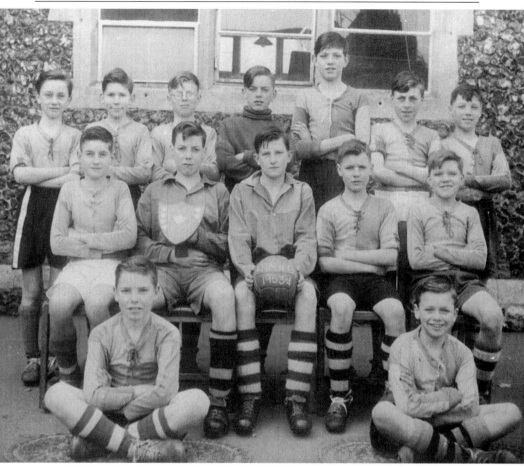

The St Dunstan's Secondary School football team, which won the Intermediate Schools Shield in the 1953/4 season. Back row, left to right: David James, David Gentle, Harold Pout, Roy Thomas, Roger Quested, Tony Blogg, Heinz Burton. Middle row: Emlyn Bond, Roy Edwards, Malcolm Longley (captain), David Jeffery, Peter Cork. Sitting on the ground: Brian Parsons, Derek Ward. In the early 1950s St Dunstan's School enjoyed a good reputation for their football teams and contested a number of finals.

The headmaster, Ronald Ratledge, with prefects at the Archbishop's Secondary School in 1959. The school opened in 1957 and was brought about by amalgamation of the Diocesan and Payne Smith Girls' School and St Dunstan's Boys' School. Back row, left to right: Sandra Butterworth, Janine Lambert, -?-, Brian Mockett, David Austin, Jimmy Tough, Roger West, John Brown. Middle row: Marilyn Collins, Jenny Clements, Pam Wood, Madeline Westover, Victor Powell, Keith Groom, Michael De'Ath, Alan Dewell. Front row: Janice Ward, Susan Glover, Heather Collinson, Sheila Todd (head girl), Mr Ratledge, John Austin (head boy), John Kloosterman, Michael Ratcliffe, Ivor Curtis.

Excavations on the site of Wincheap County Primary School by Robert Brett & Sons Ltd in 1939. The school was opened in 1940 and comprised separate buildings for juniors and infants. The junior part of the school was badly damaged in the June 1942 raids but was subsequently rebuilt. The infants' section escaped damage and was used as an emergency feeding centre. In the background are the railway embankment for the Elham Valley Line and the chimney at Frank Cooper's Lime Works.

The staff of the Wincheap County Primary School (junior department) in 1958. Back row, left to right: Messrs Vaughan, Davies, Rayner, Reid, Thompson, Hymas, Howard, Bourne, -?-. Front row: -?-, Mrs Dawes, Miss Cole, Mrs Seaman, Mr Bradshaw (headmaster), Miss Hunt, Miss Henson, Miss Moss, -?-. Cecil Bradshaw was the school's first headmaster and served in that capacity for some twenty years. He was also very much involved in the work of the Canterbury Archaeological Society.

Field-Marshal Montgomery attending a Service of Thanksgiving in October 1945 for the safe return of the King's School after its wartime evacuation to Cornwall. During the service in the Cathedral the field-marshal read the lesson and the sermon was preached by Dr Geoffrey Fisher, Archbishop of Canterbury.

St Dunstan's School pupils in 1925. The girls in the back row are: E. Wallis, Ruby Hadlow, Lily Cogger, W. Port, Lily Coultrip, Daisy Goodwin, Mary Nicholls, Irene Smith, Edie Couter, Connie Cannon, E. Belsey, Grace Overill. The boys in the front row are: Fred Croucher, Gordon Richards, Billy Beaumont, Jim Goddard, Sonny Lilley, Will Fassum, ? Dorrington, ? Webb, Ted Sears, ? Scoones, E. Harnden.

SECTION EIGHT
The Second World War

A view of the Cathedral from Burgate made possible by the blitz on Canterbury during the early hours of 1 June 1942. This 'Baedeker' raid was to devastate a great part of the St George's area and Burgate Street.

Members of the Canterbury Auxiliary Fire Service, equipped with gas masks, in Westgate Court Avenue prior to the outbreak of war in 1939. Following the setting-up of Canterbury's first National Service Committee early in 1939 under the chairmanship of the mayor, Catherine Williamson, recruits were sought both for the Canterbury Fire Brigade and the Auxiliary Fire Service. The Home Office soon asked the City Council to specify establishment for the AFS and how many people had been recruited for National Service. Progress on this front was rather slow and a number of National Service Days were held in August to encourage recruitment. During the 1939 Cricket Week the mayor did her part by entertaining those who were involved in National Service, which included members of the ARP (Air Raid Precautions), police, nursing services, the fire service, etc.

Running out the hoses, part of the training of the Auxiliary Fire Service members. On the left is the group's 'temporary' fire engine complete with ladder, facing the houses in Whitstable Road. During the blitz in June 1942 the auxiliary firemen (at that stage part of the National Fire Service) played a significant part in fighting the hundreds of fires which raged throughout the city. At a meeting soon after the blitz, Councillor J.G.B. Stone remarked that 'when he saw the fires he never thought that anything could be saved in the city. It was simply a blazing inferno. It was only by the superhuman efforts and complete disregard of danger on the part of the men who fought the fire that Canterbury was saved. Their work was beyond all praise. It was not what was lost – the miracle was what was saved. Those men delivered them from destruction.'

A section of the City of Canterbury's Fire Brigade, with their fire tender equipped with a turntable ladder, in the early years of the Second World War. In a notice published by the *Kentish Gazette* in June 1940, the chairman of the Council's Emergency Committee, Catherine Williamson (the mayor), reported that there were seventeen fire appliances available and that the city's auxiliary firemen numbered some two hundred. All of these had undergone one hundred hours of initial training.

Volunteer fire fighters equipped with stirrup-pump, hose reels and buckets, etc. in the grounds of St Augustine's College at the beginning of the Second World War. At that time St Augustine's was a missionary training college for the Anglican Communion. The imposing gateway of the college, the Fyndon Gateway, and other buildings were damaged in 1942 but were restored after the war.

Lady Wootton's Green, between Broad Street and Monastery Street, after the bombing of 1 June 1942. The houses on the right, including a timber-framed building, were so badly damaged that they had to be demolished. Thankfully, the gateway to St Augustine's College (built by Abbot Fyndon in 1309) and other college buildings were duly repaired. The gardens of Lady Wootton's Green were fully restored after the war and new houses etc. built around the green. (Reproduced with permission of the *Kent Messenger*)

St George's Street some hours after the 'Baedeker' raid devastated a large part of the city in the early hours of 1 June 1942. The premises of Marks & Spencer Ltd on the left are virtually intact, thanks largely to the construction of the building, but Barclays Bank on the opposite side of the road and the adjacent properties suffered major damage. Although the street has been cleared of debris firemen are damping down the remaining pockets of fire.

Members of the city's National Fire Service with their Standard fire engine (reg. no. AJG 500). This photograph dating from the Second World War was taken by the Herne Bay studio of F. Scrivens & Sons. The National Fire Service was founded on 18 August 1941, when the hundreds of local brigades under the control of various local authorities were brought under central control. In wartime conditions, this meant that large numbers of fire-fighting units could be moved around the country to areas under heavy attack and during the Canterbury blitz in June 1942, the new organization played a major contribution. In an interview given to the *Kent Herald* at that time, the city surveyor, Mr H.M. Enderby, paid tribute to the work of the NFS and stated that 'Many arm-chair observers, including myself, have at times been critical of the formation and personnel of the NFS. As one who loves every brick of the city I cannot but pay a warm word of appreciation to the NFS after seeing them in the height of the blitz with bombs dropping all around, doing their work so quickly and efficiently.' In its issue of the 13 June 1942 the *Kentish Gazette* paid tribute to the commander of the No. 30 (East Kent) Fire Force, Mr G.H. Robinson, who, from his headquarters near the Westgate 'stood, cool and efficient, co-ordinating and directing the activities of the hundreds of pumps. His experience in fighting fires in the London raids was invaluable and those best qualified to express an opinion were unstinted in their praise of the manner in which he did his vital job.'

Local Civil Defence personnel during the Second World War. Under the umbrella of Air Raid Precautions, members were involved in first aid and rescue parties, as ambulance drivers and air-raid wardens etc. Rescue parties consisted of ten men including the leader and driver and were often recruited from skilled tradesmen. At a meeting of the City Council just after the June blitz, Alderman Charles Lefevre remarked that 'they could congratulate themselves on the way that the leaders and members of the various Civil Defence services had carried out their duty. There was no need to refer to names – all had done their best.'

Auxiliary Fire Service members at the beginning of the Second World War after being properly equipped. They were part of the city's fire brigade before coming under control of the NFS. As volunteers for National Service they carried out their normal jobs but were expected to train and be on call for any emergency that might occur.

The demolition in 1958 of the only remaining part of the Corn and Hop Exchange or 'Long Market' that ran between St George's Street and Burgate. After severe damage in the air raids of 1 June 1942, most of the building was demolished leaving only a small section at either end. The part shown was the attractive gateway and single-storey building that housed public toilets at the Burgate end .

The City Council issued a booklet entitled *Canterbury's Problem – The Answer is Your Responsibility* early in 1945. This contained a message from the mayor, Charles Lefevre, and detailed the proposals drawn up by Dr Charles Holden, the planning consultant. Among the proposals was a plan for a Civic Way linking the Civic Centre (to be built on the site of the Council Offices adjoining the Dane John) and Burgate along the line of Marlowe Avenue and Rose Lane. The Holden Plan was fiercely opposed by the Citizen's Defence Association and most of it was subsequently abandoned. The political in-fighting that occurred at that time was mainly responsible for the delay in the rebuilding of St George's area until the early 1950s.

SECTION NINE

People

Members of the City Police being inspected by their Chief Constable, George T. Hall, outside the Pound Lane station in 1934. The Chief Constable was also the Chief Officer of the Municipal Fire Brigade.

Volunteer nurses working hard to pack medical supplies during the First World War when a number of War Hospital Supply Depots existed in the city. The blackboard on the wall records items for the Kent and Canterbury Hospital and for the British Red Cross Society for use on hospital ships sailing between Dover and Calais. During the war Voluntary Aid Detachment hospitals were located at Dane John House and Abbots Barton.

Staff of the old Kent and Canterbury Hospital in Longport, photographed by B. & W. Fisk-Moore in the 1920s. Opened in 1793, the hospital served the local population until the new building was finished in 1937. In 1925 116 beds were available and the weekly cost of an in-patient was £2 17s. The average length of stay for an in-patient was twenty days and 1,520 were admitted in that year. The number of out-patients treated in 1925 was 23,985.

William Fisk-Moore FRPS, who established his photographic business at No. 4 St George's Gate in 1905. He continued there and at No. 7 St George's Place until both premises were blitzed in the 1942 air raids, depriving him of his vast collection of pre-war negatives. After the bombing, Mr Fisk-Moore carried on his business from Lefevre's before moving to Burgate. He retired at the end of 1952 though the business carried on under his name for some years. Picture postcard collectors and all interested in Canterbury's past owe a great debt to William Fisk-Moore – much of his work has been preserved for posterity, especially his photographic record of the 1942 blitz.

The sister, Connie, of Canterbury photographer Daisy M. Pinnington, with two soldiers during the First World War. Daisy Pinnington carried on her photographic business from the time of the First World War until the late 1920s working from a studio in Wincheap, opposite the Hop Poles public house. Daisy's father, Louis, also carried out a twofold business at the same address as a cycle repairer and piano tuner.

Recruits for the army marching outside the Drill Hall in 1915. The writer of this picture postcard to his daughter asked, 'I wonder if you can see your Dad – I am drilling the recruits.' Opposite the Drill Hall stood the Sidney Cooper School of Art and Science, now the Sidney Cooper Centre. The Drill Hall was taken over by the City Council in the early 1970s for recreational use and renamed the Westgate Hall.

A group of soldiers, photographed with the rector of St Paul's church, the Revd W.L. Greene, in 1914. One of the soldiers, named Charlie, wrote home to his family at Southsea: 'Just to prove I am keeping good company here. These two old gents are our hosts at present. Fancy me being billeted with a parson. The other chap, his brother, is an Oxford Blue.'

Richard Swain (on the left) and Sidney J. 'Toby' Nash, at the old swimming baths at Whitehall, now the Toddlers' Cove, in 1929. Both were keen swimmers and taught many of Canterbury's children to swim during the 1920s. 'Toby' Nash was a skilled violinist and also a very talented artist whose many watercolour paintings of local scenes are now enthusiastically collected and command three-figure prices at auction. 'Toby' Nash died in 1960; Richard Swain, who ran the Stour Bakery, died in 1936.

Edward and Olive Solly, with their thirteen children, on the occasion of their Silver Wedding on 19 February 1935. A local newspaper described Mr Solly as 'Canterbury's Happiest Married Man' and the *Daily Mirror* carried a report and photograph, quoting Mr Solly: 'I'm lucky, I just happen to have the best wife in the world.' Mr Solly became licensee of the Kentish Cricketers inn during 1908 and remained there until 1941.

A Victorian baker photographed by James Craik, an electric light portrait produced in his 'Electric and Daylight' Studios at No. 51 Burgate Street and No. 33 St Margaret's Street. At this time you could have your portrait taken and purchase a dozen cartes-de-visite for 6s with 'no extra charges'. In 1889 Mr Craik moved his studio to No. 4 St George's Gate, opposite the cattle market, where he was 'patronised by H.R.H. The Prince of Wales, Prince Napoleon Murat and Duchess D'Alencon.'

An outing to a local brewery, probably the Dane John Brewery, c. 1930. The group are men, mainly from the Ickham and Wickhambreaux area, who were customers of the Unicorn public house at Bekesbourne. It includes Messrs Fox, Young, Allen, Whybourne, Fagg, Fittall (two), E. Moon, Buggins, Masters, Justice, Gambrill, Marsh, P. Moon, Addley, Clarke, Rudd, Hussey, Pilcher (two), Cornwell, Tucker, Bushell and Sayer.

A carnival float featuring the Stephen Langton Lodge, No. 1659, of the International Order of Good Templars. The photograph, which dates from the early part of this century, was actually taken in Harwich Street, Whitstable. This 'Friendly and Benefit Society' met at the Rechabites Hall in Pound Lane and was one of many such societies in the city. Stephen Langton was the forty-third Archbishop of Canterbury when he was appointed in 1207.

Members of the Ancient Order of Druids, Canterbury – Lodge No. 98 – taking part in a carnival procession in the 1920s. Up until the First World War this lodge met at the Seven Stars public house in Orange Street but after that war moved to the Bell Hotel in High Street. In the 1930s the lodge was known as the 'Durovernum'.

The Rescue Section of the Canterbury Division of the Civil Defence Corps after winning a competition at Maidstone, *c.* 1960. The group, which was in opposition to other units from the county, was led by its senior officer, George Cox. Back row, left to right: Sidney Hooper, Johnny Horn, George Cox, Stanley Mercer, Fred Acott, -?-. Front row: Bill Middleton, Sidney Lamb, Gerry Page, Bill Gray. Back in October 1944, Jack Skelton the local Civil Defence Officer, suggested that social and welfare activities should continue after the cessation of hostilities. The arrival of the cold war and the threat of atomic warfare ensured that the civil defence organization continued in its vital role for some years to come.

Catherine Williamson at the time of the 1945 General Election when she stood as a Common Wealth candidate in the Canterbury constituency. Mrs Williamson was first elected to the City Council in 1934 and became the city's first woman mayor in 1938. During her two year's mayoralty she played a vital role in organizing the city's Civil Defence forces and acted as chairman of the Emergency Committee in the first year of the Second World War. After the 1942 blitz she was appointed organizing secretary for Mayor Charles Lefevre's Air Raid Distress Fund. The account of the wartime years in Canterbury in her book *Though the Streets Burn* is an outstanding record of those times.

Edward Heath, the Leader of the Opposition, at the University of Kent's Rutherford College for a 'Questions and Answers' session in February 1967. Accompanying Mr Heath is David Nunnerley. Behind Mr Heath is Dr Harry Cragg, currently Dean of Natural Sciences at the university. Rutherford College, designed by William Holford & Partners, was the university's second college, built in 1966. It is of interest to observe that the university opened in 1965, thirty-three years after a Mr F. Carson, speaking at the reopening of the Canterbury Evening School, said 'I believe Canterbury ought to have its own University.'

Acknowledgements

Once again I am most grateful to a number of people who readily loaned photographs to supplement my own material. In particular I wish to thank Neil Mattingly for allowing me to reproduce some of his fine collection of picture postcards, Ted Yeoman for the loan of photographs depicting the transport of C. & G. Yeoman, and Jim Styles for the use of a number of his photographs dating from the 1960s and 1970s. My thanks are also due to the following for the loan of and/or permission to use an assortment of postcards and photographs:

Ted Abbott • David Alexander • Olive and George Anderson
Charles Bentley • Tony Blake • Joan Bluck • Allan Butler • Cliff Court
Doris Cox • Dot Gilder • Len Grace • Ella Grundy • Colin Hadler
Maurice Hart • Gilbert Lawrence • Eleanor Overill • Eric Pettit
Richard Phipps • Revd Samuel Reading • Denis Reding • Jack Snell
Pat Spence and Madge Wenham.

Many people, too numerous to mention, assisted me with information for the captions and I am grateful to Alan Bensted, group editor of the *Kent Messenger*, for permission to reproduce newspaper photographs which first appeared in the *Kentish Gazette* and *Kentish Express*. David Cousins, the reference librarian, and his staff at the Canterbury Library were again very helpful in my quest for information and the recently created Local Studies Room proved most useful. Tony Blake and Jim Styles were of great help to me in the processing of photographic prints from a variety of originals and their efforts are much appreciated.

Finally, my thanks go to Margaret Smyth for reading the captions and to my wife, Isabel, for typing the manuscripts and providing invaluable assistance in many other ways.